Walkir our Heritage in Essex

George Hassan PhD.[Lond].

First published 1999 by
Dr George Hassan.
Orchard House, Main Road, Ford End, Chelmsford,
Essex CM3 1LL.

Email: dr.george.hassan@cwcom.net

ISBN 0 9535908 0 1

A catalogue record for this book is available from the British Library

Printed and bound in Great Britain by
M&B (FELSTED) Ltd.
M&B House, Chelmsford Road Industrial Estate,
Dunmow, Essex CM6 1HD

By the same author:
Building Services 1996, [Macmillan Press Ltd.].
Spanish Version, [A. Madrid Vicente, Ediciones].

I DEDICATE THIS BOOK to MY WIFE

Joy.

[For whom this will be a 'first'].

'To be fond of knowledge is better than simply acquiring it and to take delight in it is far better than simply being fond of it.'

Confucius circa 551 - 479 BC

Contents

List of Walks

Key:

One route---R
Choice of two routes-------------------------------2R
Choice of four routes------------------------------ 4R

Illustrations

Cover illustration of the Clock House – Great Dunmow,
(with the permission of Mr and Mrs Stile)
by: **Margaret Pedlar**

Other illustrations by:
Jimmy Johns
John Johnson
Margaret Pedlar
Peter Vincett.

Photograph of the 'Waltham Wanderers'
on Dick Nunn's Bridge at Coggeshall by: **Peter Jackson.**

List of Illustrations

Key:
Watercolour---------------------------------------W
Pen and ink drawing---------------------------- P
Photograph------------------------------------ PH
Coloured diagram------------------------------ CD

Note

All walks are undertaken at the walker's own risk. At the time of publication all the routes shown on the sketch maps and described in the text, followed public rights of way and permitted paths. Sometimes however diversions do take place and permissions are rescinded. In the event, the publisher cannot be held responsible for any information given on the sketch maps, or in the text, which then becomes inaccurate. Neither can he be held responsible for any damage caused by members of the public tresspassing on private property as a result of such changes, or for any other reason.

Preface

All of the walks start and finish in the same place and, in an attempt to cater for 'mixed ability' groups, the routes have been designed so that in nearly all of the walks those taking part can choose to opt for the 'prescribed' walk, or for the 'shorter' walk, as they wish.

The book is small enough to slip easily into the pocket of an anorak, so that it should not be too difficult to consult the sketch map and the text for each walk; however it is suggested that the prose relating to the historical details might with advantage be read before embarking on the walk. In this way it should then be possible to enjoy the countryside, with only an occasional reference to the relevant sketch map; hopefully avoiding stepping into a rabbit hole while reading!

For those who are venturing to walk along footpaths for the first time, it should be mentioned that the perceived route of a footpath (particularly when it crosses a field), will appear to change slightly with the farming calendar. Usually after harvest the farmer ploughs his fields and between the time it takes to do this and subsequently to level the ground, it is not unusual for the route of the footpath to be less than clear. Lore has it that after such work the path should be reinstated and, generally this does appear to be done. In practice it is unrealistic to expect the 're-walking' of the footpath to be carried out instantaneously and this does mean that at certain times of the year, walkers can expect to have to negotiate freshly ploughed fields, which may even consist of muddy Essex clay!

Readers will notice that in most cases I have avoided giving detailed notes as to the directions to be taken along the routes, believing that it is infinitely better for walkers to find their own way at each of the turning points, which in most instances are well marked with footpath and other signs. Generally, where guidance is needed, the information will be found in the text.

In none of the 10 walks described is it necessary for walkers to be as proficient as those who walk in mountainous or moorland areas, which may at any time become shrouded in mist. However as it is always desirable to be able to set up one's own elementary checks as to the intended direction of the walk, I have described how this can be done with the aid of a map and a walker's compass in **Appendix A.**

For those who wish to obtain further information on 'route finding' with map and compass, of a standard suitable for use in potentially hazardous situations; such as those which might be encountered on an exploration designed to comply with the standards required by the Duke of Edindurgh's Award, I would refer them to Wally Keay's book entitled 'Land Navigation'.

Throughout the text I have made use of the National grid reference system to 'pinpoint' places of historical interest and to specify the starting point of each walk. For those readers who are not familiar with this code, an explanation and an example are given in **Appendix B.**

When quoting from old writings I have done so as accurately as modern typescript allows. Some readers may not be familiar with the use of the old typescript found in old prose, whereby sometimes (but not always), the letter 's' is printed as an 'eff' having a short crossbar on the left hand side of the symbol and, the letter 'f' is printed as a modern day 'f' with a full crossbar. As far as I can discover there does not seem to be a rule as to when an 's' should be written as the 'eff' symbol with a short crossbar. For instance in the Reverend Philip Morant's 'History and Antiquities of the County of Essex', the word 'Suffolk' is printed as it is today. Whereas 'sons' is printed having the first letter represented by the 'eff' symbol with a short crossbar and with the last letter as an 's'.

The keyboard of my computer does not have an 'eff' symbol with a short crossbar, so that when quoting from old writings and carvings I have automatically typed an 'f', which in some cases does seem to have resulted in my producing copy that might be considered worthy of one of Ronny Barker's sketches, - for which of course no apologies should ever be needed!

Acknowledgements

Research

The subject matter for this book required a good deal of research and I was ably assisted in this by the staff of the Essex Record Office, who unstintingly offered their own personal brand of expertise in pointing me towards those sections of the archives which were most likely to be of use.

Thanks are also due to Ms Alison Bennett for guiding me through the system used by the County Town Planners, in their Department of 'Sites and Monuments' at Chelmsford.

Many other people offered information and whenever appropriate, due acknowledgements have been made in the text.

Prose

Clearly any book must be written in a way which is (hopefully) acceptable to the most demanding of readers and, I have been helped in this particular endeavour firstly by my wife, who willingly undertook to read my first drafts, subsequently pointing me (always with great tact), towards better ways of expression; and secondly, by a 'Mistress of English' Mrs Jill Mitchell, who in spite of a heavy recurring marking schedule was always willing to act as the final checker and arbiter in matters involving the written word. I thank them both.

Practice

Any book containing practical instructions has to have those instructions checked by others and in this instance, each of the 10 walks described was first walked by myself and then subsequently amended and re-walked, before trying them and the associated text out on our local walking club, known worldwide as the `Waltham Wanderers'. Initially this stratagem resulted in some members of the club acting as unsuspecting (but very well informed), guinea pigs! However an inbuilt sense of fairness on my part soon put that right and in addition, I now find myself in a position to thank them publicly for their (initial) forebearance.

Happy walking!

George Hassan. **Chelmsford, Essex. 1999.**

Pleshey and the Castle remains

Walk 1

THE name of Pleshey was first mentioned in 1144 as 'Plaseiz'. The name is Norman-French in origin and according to Reaney the word signified an enclosure which was often forested and enclosed by a coppiced hedge. Before that the town was known as Tumbelstoun, or the town of Tumuli or Hills [1]. As a matter of interest Julius Caesar described a British town as:

> *"a tract of woody country surrounded by a mound and a ditch, (built) for the security of themselves and their cattle against the incursions of their enemies."*

Pleshey is just such a place; only nowadays it is, of course, referred to as being a village. It is surrounded by a semi-circular bank and ditch which it is believed was made after 1167 by the owner William de Mandeville who had been given permission to refortify the castle.

Pleshey Castle remains

The construction of the earthworks of Pleshey Castle is hybrid. They are the result of work done by the ancient Britons and the subsequent efforts of the Romans, Danes and Normans [1]. To date, no evidence has been found of Saxon occupation and Pleshey is not mentioned in the Domesday Book. The particular type of construction is referred to as 'Motte and Bailey' and that at Pleshey is considered to be one of the finest examples of this type of castle construction in Britain. An account of the way in which the Town Enclosure, the Motte and lower and upper Baileys came into being, may be found in reference[2]. Pottery dating from prehistoric times has been found in the castle bailey and the site may have been ploughed since at least the Iron age [3].

During the medieval period it was home to the de Mandevilles and the de Bohuns who were High Constables of England. In 1380 the castle passed by marriage to Thomas of Woodstock, the first duke of Gloucester, who was the uncle of Richard II. In 1420 Pleshey was acquired by Henry V and later it formed part of the marriage-portion of the Queens of England. The castle was kept in repair under the auspices of both Henry VI and Edward VI, but after the death of King Edward in 1553 it fell to ruin [4].

It is fortunate that the brick built bridge leading from the southern bailey up to the highest part of the castle is still in existence and has been kept in good repair over the years by the late Mr J J Tufnell of Langleys at Great Waltham and his descendants, whose family has owned the land since 1720 and continues so to do.

The bridge which is unique in Britain is one of only two in Europe of that date [4]. It was constructed circa 1450 when Margaret Countess of Richmond (the mother of Henry VII) was living at the Castle. The bridge was mentioned in a survey carried out in 1558-9 when it was already considered to be 'old'. Another part of the same survey was carried out on the area in front of the brick bridge (the southern bailey) and the results indicated that it contained (albeit in ruins) a hall, various houses, the Constable's House, a kitchen, the outer gatehouse and a chapel, some of which have been identified by subsequent excavations.

The highest part of the castle motte was excavated in 1907 by Colonel W N Tufnell who discovered a rectangular building having external dimensions of 17 x 20 m. Three different types of construction were found and it is thought (by Rahtz), that this could have been the 15th century Great Hall which is described in earlier documentation. Eight Roman coins were found representative of the reigns of

Claudius II, Victorinus and Tetricus Senior, together with a Roman brooch.

Subsequent excavations carried out by S R Bassett (1972-74, 1977-78 and 1980) to the east of the brick bridge revealed some flint rubble support piers for an earlier timber bridge which was dated to the late 12th or early 13th century, together with a medieval timber framed building with domestic outhouses. Also, when digging at the bailey bank, the earliest period yielded some fourth century Roman pottery including much Hadham ware [5].

A well documented period of history pertaining to the castle took place during the reign of King Richard II from 1377 to 1399. Richard was made King when he was only 11 years old and in his early years the kingdom was governed by his uncles, John of Gaunt and the Dukes of Lancaster and Gloucester. As Richard grew older he began to associate with favourites of his own age, whom he would gratify solely to further his and their own common pleasures; which unfortunately were sometimes seen to be at the expense of his Kingly duties. The following excerpt taken from Gower's 'Character of Richard II' sums up the situation:

> *"The foolish council of the lewde and young he did receive, and grave advice of aged heads he did reject and leave."*

Such behaviour became irksome to his uncles and in 1386 they reacted by setting up 'A New Regency', of which the Duke of Gloucester was head, effectively stripping the King of all his power. Predictably judges were found who pronounced the Regency as treasonable, and the Duke of Gloucester and his associates then took action by putting to death some of Richard's favourites, including a much loved tutor. However when the king reached his 23rd year he declared himself 'old enough to govern'; his uncles were dismissed and the Regency was then ignored.

Seven years later Richard entered into a family alliance with the French King by marrying his daughter, who at that

Ancient Brick Bridge Pleshey Castle

time was a child of seven! The towns of Brest (once captured by the Earl of Arundel) and Cherbourg, were given to Brittany and it was even rumoured that Calais, which had been in English hands since 1347 would also be relinquished. The Duke of Gloucester who had earnt his 'spurs' by performing valiant/ dastardly deeds while at war with the French, became increasingly alarmed and decided that Richard should be removed from the throne and be confined for life. He was to be replaced by the heir apparent, (the elder son of John of Gaunt), and the war with France was to be resumed, with the administration of the kingdom being divided between the Earl of Arundel and himself.

The inevitable 'leak' occurred and a counter plot was hatched in which both the Earl of Arundel and the Duke of Gloucester were to be seized. According to reference [6], Richard's part in this involved his riding from Havering-atte-Bower where he was staying, to Pleshey, where he knew he would find his uncle at his well appointed home in Pleshey Castle.

Richard's arrival was both late in the day and unexpected and the Duke and his family had already finished their evening meal; however the King and his party were given food and refreshments and again according to reference[6], Richard is quoted as saying:

> *"Fair Uncle, cause five or six of your horses to be saddled, for I will pray you to ride with me to London to discuss important matters of State."*

The party duly set off from the Castle for London, when almost certainly they would have used the bridleways to the South of Pleshey which connect with the Roman road passing through Brentwood, Romford and Stratford. These bridleways have been defined by reference [1], as taking in Letfield Lane along which the present walk is routed. The King had arranged for an ambush to take place near Stratford and on approaching the area he galloped ahead; his uncle was then seized, taken to Calais and then imprisoned in the Castle for two months. During this time the Duke confessed to the charges laid against him and then pleaded with Richard cogently but unsuccessfully for his life, using the following words:

> *"I beseche to his heygh lordeschippe that he wyll, for the passion that God suffered for all mankynde, and the compassion that He hadde for His moder on the cross, and the pitye that He hadde of Marye Maudeleyne, that he will vouchesauf to have compassion and pityee and to accept me unto his mercy and to his grace, as he that hath ever bene ful of mercy and grace to all his lieges, and to all other that have naght bene so neygh unto hym as I have bene, though I be unworthy"*

Subsequent events show that Richard was not swayed from his purpose and the Duke was taken to the 'Prince's Inn' in Calais and suffocated between two feather beds by six servants, who according to reference[1] had earlier that morning been sworn to secrecy by the Earl of Nottingham in the Church of Notre Dame. Conveniently the Duke was reported to have died of apoplexy on September 17th 1398 in his 45th year; but the true circumstances of the deed were later uncovered by one of the guilty men making a confession, for which he was subsequently hanged.

King Richard took control of Pleshey castle and later removed almost everything of any value from both the Castle and the Church at Pleshey. The complete sets of armour belonging to the Duke of Gloucester, the Earl of Arundel and of Thomas Earl of Warwick were ordered to be sent to the Tower by a writ of privy seal dated November 22nd 1398.

They consisted of chain mail, conical helmets, coats of arms, trappers for the horses, swords, daggers and lances. An inventory was made (in French), by members of the King's Treasury, and we are indebted to the authors of reference [7] for an English translation of this.

Part of the inventory consisted of 14-carpets, the sizes of which varied from 20 yd long by 4 yd wide to 10 yd long by 4 yd wide, with three of these consisting of 'blue Arras powdered with yellow garters'; tapestry hangings referred to as 'Cloths of Arras' from the Hall and Chambers; hangings from six beds, one of which is described as follows:

> *"A great bed of gold, that is to say a coverlet, a tester (or canopy) and the entire celure (or valance) of fine blue satin wrought with garters of gold, and three curtains of tartaryn beaten to match. Also two long and four square pillows of the set of the bed"*.

Among the items taken from the wardrobes were eight gowns lined or faced with minever or other fur and a gown of red velvet. The library consisted of 84 volumes. The Chapel vestments included 75 different items which included Bishops' cloaks, altar cloths, two silver candelsticks weighing 4 lb 3 1/2 oz, a holy water container and sprinkler of silver gilt weighing 3 lb 2 1/2 oz and a censer (or thurible), with silver chains.

The Dukes widow, Eleanor, was clearly much troubled at this time; over a period of one year she had witnessed the death of her husband in suspicious circumstances, the looting of her very well appointed Castle and Chapel, and also (unfortunately), the death of her only son. She died broken-hearted a few months later. William Shakespeare in Richard II, commemorated her feelings in Act 1 scene 2 with Eleanor saying:

> "---Farewell, old Gaunt: thy sometimes brother's wife with her companion grief must end her life."

Another quote from the same source (Eleanor speaking):

> "-------------------------------*Bid him-ah, what?-*

With all good speed at Plashy visit me.
Alack, and what shall good old York there see,
But empty lodgings and unfurnish'd walls,
Unpeopled offices, untrodden stones?
And what cheer there for welcome, but my groans?
Therefore commend me; let him not come there,
To seek out sorrow that dwells everywhere.
Desolate, desolate will I hence and die:
The last leave of thee takes my weeping eye."

Holy Trinity Church

The church was built in happier times by Eleanor's husband Thomas Woodstock (Duke of Gloucester), as a thanksgiving for his deliverance from a particularly violent storm which occurred in the English Channel, when he was returning from one of his military expeditions in France. The Duke averred that if he was spared from drowning he would set up a religious foundation or college, which would be dedicated to the Holy Trinity. This was accomplished and Richard II licensed the College of Canons in 1394. The college buildings and glebe land occupied an area of 6 acres to the south west of the present churchyard and it is still referred to as 'The Holy Land' [8].

One of the rules of the College was that it was to have no female members; however if by 'some unavoidable account' it was found that women had to be admitted to its buildings they were to be 'women of character'. Clearly such a loosely worded stricture was intended to cover all conceivable eventualities.

The lower part of the church tower and probably the foundations of the transepts are the remaining parts of the collegiate church and these form the core of the present building [4]. A small stone referred to as the 'Pleshey Stone' and inscribed 'RICARDUS REX II' has been set in the wall of the choir vestry in the north transept and according to information catalogued by the Archaeological section of Chelmsford's Town Planning department, it was at one time built in to a wall at Mount House. It is believed to indicate royal possession of Pleshey Castle after the death of the Duke of Gloucester in1397.

In 1546 in common with many other religious establishments throughout the country the College was taken over by Henry VIII. He then gave it to his Captain of the Guard Sir John Gate, who then proceeded to 'asset strip' the Castle, the College and the Church. The Chancel of the church was demolished and it was at this point in an attempt to preserve their place of worship that the parishioners purchased the remaining body of the church, which included the steeple and the two original bells. Almost two centuries of gradual decay followed, until in 1720 Pleshey Manor was purchased by Sir William Joliffe of London and Ewell[10]. His nephew Samuel Tufnell then repaired the tower of the church and rebuilt the Chancel, creating at the same time a family vault.

Most of the dwellings in The Street can also be dated to this time.

In 1862 more work was commissioned by John Joliffe Tufnell and the vicar of that time the Reverend J Hutchinson. This changed the architectural style of the church to its present one of Victorian neo-gothic. Over the years three extra bells were added, one in 1620, one in 1752 and the last one in 1854.

Details of Walk 1

Map required:

Ordnance Survey Pathfinder Map No.1098 (TL 61/71) Great and Little Waltham 1:25 000.

Starting and finishing point:

Pleshey village hall Grid Reference TL 662 143.

Walking with our Heritage - Pleshey

The prescribed walk following the red arrows
Distance covered:
9.6 km (5.9 miles).
Duration of walk:
3 h 30 min. including a 30min break
Condition of Terrain:
A good proportion of the walk takes place on bridleways so that hoof prints and the inevitable large ruts caused by farm machinery will be encountered. These should not concern inveterate walkers, but in wet weather a little extra time should be allowed for those members of a mixed ability group who have not yet gained their 'spurs'!

The shorter walk following the green arrows
Distance covered:
5.5 km (3.4 miles)
Duration of walk:
2 h 15 min. including a 30 minute break
Condition of terrain:
Generally firm and relatively smooth.

Places of refreshment:
The White Horse and the Leather Bottle in Pleshey, the Pig and Whistle 1.0 km (0.62 mile) south west of Beadle's cross, grid reference TL 679 111.

For the origin of the name 'Pig and Whistle' see the end of the text.

The first part of the walk takes a route around the mound and ditch to the North of Pleshey which formed part of the refortification carried out just after 1167 by William de Mandeville.

At the junction of The Street and Back Lane at grid reference TL 6659 1460, the remains of a timber palisade consisting of 18 in x 10 in squared oak baulks was discovered forming a line across the main street. These are now kept in Colchester museum and dendrochronological dating gave a time span for the timber of 1110 ± 5 AD.

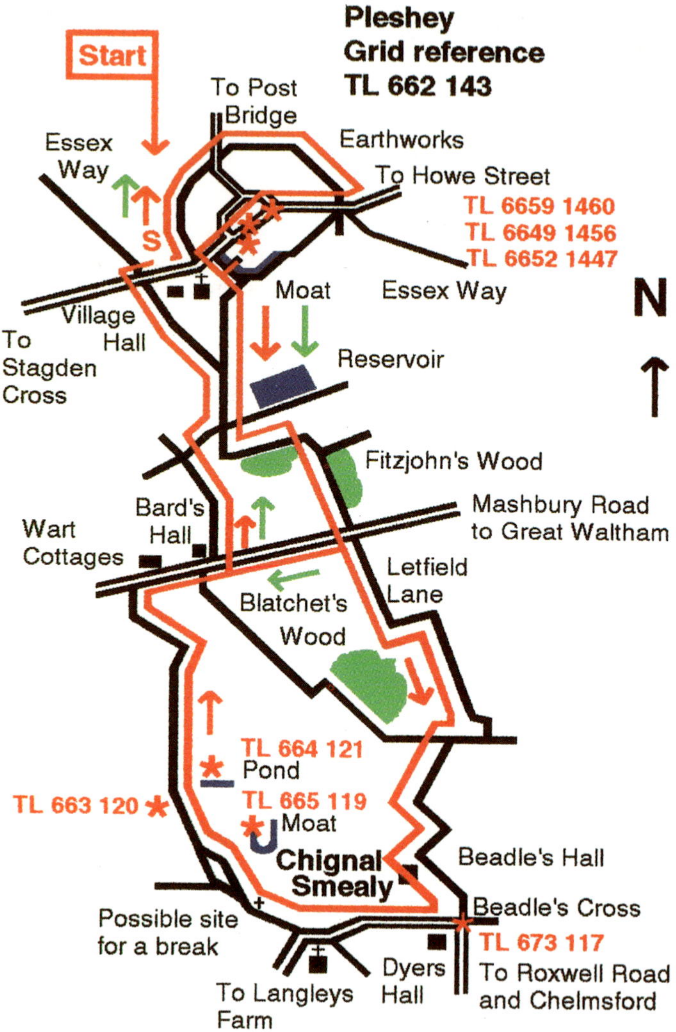

* - Position of dig with grid reference

S - Starting point for both walks. For the prescribed walk follow the red arrows. For the shorter walk follow the green arrows.

Walk 1

Continuing through the village along The Street, the site of the old market place (grid reference TL 6649 1456), is on the north side of the road level with 'The Gardens' Cottage. The market ceased to function around the beginning of the 18th century.

The road leading to the Castle entrance is on the left and is called Pump Lane. A short distance along this lane an opening on the left leads across a bridge and over the moat to the present and late medieval entrance to the Castle earthworks. The Motte and southern bailey may be seen together with the brick bridge. Entrance to the Castle grounds is by appointment and details are given on a sign at the entrance to Pump Lane.

The walk continues past Fitzjohn's Wood and along Letfield Lane and it is just possible that it was along this route that the plundered contents of Pleshey Castle would have been transported (see the note about the route to London in the next section).

There are some large pieces of stone outside Beadles Hall which it is conjectured might once have formed the base for supporting Beadle's Cross [5]. The cross once stood at the junction of three or four ways as shown on the sketch map.

On the return journey to Pleshey the walk continues from Beadle's Cross, through Chignall Smealy, shortly after which the sketch map indicates a possible site for a break.

The moat shown on the sketch map is 10 m wide x 2 m deep and an iron cauldron and pottery dating from the 14th to the 15th century have been found in the area. In the area north east of the pond at Bereman's Farm, Belgic black coarse ware has been unearthed. Also at a point close to the bridle way at grid reference TL 663 120 Roman pottery has been uncovered.

The route taken on this return section past Wart Cottages and Bards Hall, includes a large proportion of bridleways eventually connecting with Essex Way, which on this particular section is more than wide enough to allow wagons and coaches travelling in different directions to pass each other. During bad weather it would have been necessary to have alternative routes available for the transportation of goods and people between Pleshey Castle and London and it is likely that the return part of this walk would have served as just such an alternative route.

The Route to London Southwards from Beadle's Cross.

As a matter of interest reference [1] mentions that the path to London carried on from Beadle's Cross, Southwards along the road from Chignal Smealy, past the present Pig and Whistle public house into the Roxwell road, which it passed over to a ford in the meadows and thence into the Chelmsford road at Widford at grid reference TL 695 050. This road (now classified as the B1002), is referred to as the 'Great (Roman) Road' by Miller Christy in reference [9], and it must also be noted that in this latter reference a Roman loop road is mentioned as branching off the Great Road from Margaretting at grid reference TL 667 015, via Writtle to Chelmsford, where it joins the Roman road from Braintree. Christy records that of all the Roman roads which he has catalogued in his book this loop road is the least well defined. He goes on to conclude that while it is possible that travellers to London in 1398 might have followed this route, it may well have fallen into decay before that time.

The origin of the name 'Pig and Whistle'

The name is a corruption of a 'peg o'wassail'. 'Wassail' deriving from Old Norse 'ves heill' meaning 'be in good health'. According to the Collins English Dictionary the word also has roots in Old English 'wes hale' (heil) meaning be healthy and robust. The word 'peg' is a reference to the small pegs of horn which were used as markers on the insides of leather drinking vessels to indicate when a certain volume of beer had been poured. Hence the phrase 'to take someone down a peg or two', means that their leather drinking vessel would only be partially filled to the level of the lower pegs.

References

Most of the references may be found in the 'Pleshey Castle box', held in the Essex Record Office in Chelmsford.

1 A short history of Pleshey; Its Lords and its Antiquities Written at Pleshey Parsonage in 1864.

2 The Essex Record Office publication 'Pleshey Castle, A guide to the parts of the Castle'.

3 The History and Antiquities of Pleshey 1803 Essex Record Office T/P81

4 Maria Medleycott. Pleshey: Historic Towns Project Assessment report March 1998 The Archaeology Section, Essex County Council Planning Department, County Hall, Chelmsford.

5 The Archaeology Section, Essex County Council Planning Department, County Hall, Chelmsford.

6 Lucy Menzies Pleshey: Notes on the History of its earthworks its Castle and College of the Holy Trinity Circa 1930.

7 Inventory of the Goods and Chattels belonging to Thomas Duke of Gloucester communicated by Viscount Dillon and W. St. John Hope. Reprinted by The Archaeological Journal September 1897.

8 Stuart Mole. A short history of Holy Trinity Pleshey, obtainable from the Church.

9 Transactions of the Essex Archaeological Society vol XV. New Series 1921, Miller Christy on Roman Roads in Essex, pps 201-2 (Route 2).

10 Verbal and documentary information given by Mrs David Micklem and Mr Alexander Micklem of Langleys.

Great and Little Leighs

Walk 2

Leez Priory

THE Augustinian priory was established circa 1200 by Sir Ralph Gernon. The foundations of the Priory and Chapels are still in existence and a plan of these is given in reference [1]. The sketch map shows the sites of the remains of fish ponds which were at one time stocked with trout and which were supplied from the river Ter, (which was rerouted 50 to 100 years ago), but still crosses the site. The ponds were constructed by the monks and may have doubled as mill ponds so that in times of drought the Priory mill could still keep operating. According to Morant one of the three fine parks which were appended to the Priory in the time of Lord Rich was called Pond Park after the Fish ponds and it covered an area of 413 acres.

The influence of the Priory spread to other Counties, and the monks were able to adopt a life style commensurate with the importance of their establishment, gratifying all their various and seemingly sometimes nefarious needs. This state of affairs did not go unnoticed and in 1309, the Prior invited Bishop Baldock to carry out a tour of inspection and to issue a series of injunctions, intended to cover the future personal conduct of the monks [2]. A selection from these injunctions follows and the reader may find it interesting to read between the lines.

Walking with our Heritage
Great and Little Leighs

> *"---the diligent visitation of every part of the House by the sub-prior or president; infringement of the rule of silence to be punished by two days of bread and water diet; the exclusion of women; the abstaining from ever going into the wood, the town or elsewhere without leave of the prior, and then only with an honest companion; the forbidding of any individual canon giving his food or fragments from the table to boys or others outside the refectory;---."*

In spite of these injunctions the subsequent existence of the monks at Great Leez could not have been too fraught, as they and those who followed them continued to inhabit the site for the next 200 years until 1536, when they became victims of King Henry VIII's greatest acquisitorial confidence trick, the 'Dissolution of the Monasteries'.

In England at that time the religious establishments owned approximately 25% of the cultivated land, together with many artefacts, some of which contained jewels and precious metals. Henry, faced with the pressing task of raising money to support a war against France, combined with his frustration at not being granted yet another divorce by the Pope, led him to decide that a pertinent solution to his problems would be to seize the monastic buildings, confiscate their considerable riches, and sell their lands.

In an attempt to make such a bold concept appear even minimalistically reasonable, four lieutenants under the command of Thomas Cromwell were instructed to visit, as a matter of urgency, every religious establishment in England to ascertain whether or not the moral conduct of the incumbents could be considered to be above reproach! Curiously the county of Lincolnshire was not included in the survey [1]; could money have changed hands between the lieutenants and the monks of Lincolnshire, or were Henry's representatives merely expediting the survey, as originally required?

Leez Priory

One of the first of the smaller establishments to be 'dissolved' was that at Leez. The monks were re-established in Waltham Abbey, the contents of the Priory sold and the buildings demolished. An inventory of the time showed that Lord Rich took possession of the contents of the kitchens and some 'feather beddes'.

Richard Ryche (Lord Rich), was a lawyer and a staunch Puritan. Initially he was commended to Thomas Cromwell, who subsequently recommended him to King Henry, who "admired his distinct reasoning" [4].

According to the same reference:

> *"Queen Anne Bullen (Boleyn), was taken with his graceful eloquence, and ingenious discourse; in the morning his pliant soul, that could answer all the turnings and windings of business, was as reserved and solid as that of a demure statesman; in the evening, as cheerful and merry as that of a debonair courtier. He has the wisdom of the court in the prescence, and its wit in the closet; its oracle there, and its pleasure here."*

Lord Rich subsequently became Solicitor General and also Chancellor of the Court of Augmentation, which dealt with the order in which the monasteries were to be appropriated. In May 1536 the King granted the site of the Priory and various other possessions including the Manors of Great and Little Leighs, Felsted and Fyfield to Lord Rich. Reference [4] refers to Thomas Cromwell as being "the MAWL and Rich the HAMMER of the Abbeys". It may also be noted that it was the deposition of Lord Rich which outmanoeuvred Sir Thomas More when he was being accused of refusing to recognise the divine right of kings, in particular that of Henry VIII.

Lord Rich was a great builder and he commenced the construction of a mansion on the site of the Priory after the style of Hampton Court, with buildings which surrounded two courtyards. Access to the main courtyard was effected by passing through an outer gate house and, progression to the second courtyard was via an inner gate house, both of which are still in existence.

It is known that Queen Elizabeth I travelled a great deal, engaging in 'progresses' through the Eastern Counties. On these occasions she stayed at many of the grander country houses and castles and according to reference[1], the queen's entourage would consist typically of 20 coaches, 300 baggage carts and numerous riding horses! It is easy to appreciate that the cost to the owner of the establishment favoured by such a visit was not miniscule and it is on record that when she visited Leez Priory in 1561, the overall cost of her stay amounted to more than four times the price Lord Rich paid for the development of the property. Elizabeth visited the Priory on two other occasions in 1571 and again in 1579.

Lord Rich founded Felsted Grammar School and when he died in 1567 he was interred in the East Chapel of Felsted church in a canopied tomb topped by a carved reclining effigy. A pen and ink sketch of this is given. His eldest son, Sir Robert Rich on becoming the second baron, purchased the hereditary title of the Earl of Warwick from James I, and his statue (somewhat hacked about by those who specialise in wrecking the painstaking work of others), may be seen in a kneeling position beside the tomb.

In 1619 the eldest son of Robert, also (confusingly) named Robert Rich inherited the title, becoming the second Earl and during his lifetime he became Speaker of the House of Commons, the Lord Lieutenant of Essex and the Lord High Admiral of the Fleet. He was a friend of Oliver Cromwell and was also a staunch Puritan. He was instrumental in helping to colonise New England and to this day there is a 'Lord Rich' Society in America, some of whose members have visited Felsted church and claim to be descended from the Rich family. The second Earl presided over the Justices of the Peace at Chelmsford Assizes and in this role was responsible

The Tomb of Lord Rich - Founder of Felsted School

for promulgating many trials of witches, some of whom were taken from areas in and around Great and Little Leighs.

The treatment and trials of witches in Essex.

The county of Essex had the dubious honour of having a higher incidence of witch trials than the counties of Hertfordshire and Kent and Surrey and Sussex combined and in 1645, out of 29 women who were tried, 19 received the death sentence. Witch trials in Essex extended from 1558-1678 reaching a peak of 68 cases in the decade from 1578-1587. The next highest peak of 45 prosecutions occurred between 1638 and 1647 and these were brought about by the combined talents of the second Earl (Robert Rich), and a witch finder and persecutor par excellence called Mathew Hopkins, who was referred to as the 'Witchfinder General'.

Mathew Hopkins' first 'crusade' against witches took place in and around the village of Great Leighs [3]. He was helped in this work by a team of fellow travellers whose names subsequently appeared fairly frequently as witnesses for the prosecution at the trials which were conducted at Chelmsford Assizes.

It was customary for any suspect witch to be made to sit cross-legged on a stool or table in the middle of a room (bound if necessary), and then kept without food and sleep for 24 hours. A hole would be made in the door of the room, so that any or all of the 'imps' belonging to the witch, could have access to her during her time of privation. During this period the victim was watched, so that when in desperation she 'summoned her impes to suck,' the observers would be aware of the situation! The watchers were exhorted to sweep the room on a regular basis, killing all spiders and flies; those insects which managed to escape from being killed, were then by default, automatically deemed to be the witch's imps. Such was the 'modus operandi' of Mathew

Hopkins and friends and clearly success in these endeavours was guaranteed!

It is a common belief that witches were always burnt at the stake, but in fact most were hanged. The exceptions are thought to have occurred because they were found guilty of heresy, poisoning or treason; however under Act 22 of Henry VIII, the act of poisoning was made treasonable and was then punishable by 'deth by boylynge'. Such an act would require a very large and consequently very heavy iron pot, probably only obtainable on loan from the kitchens of a large establishment. Faced with such a request it is relevant to question how many competent cooks would contemplate the task of cleaning such a pot after it was returned, ready for its subsequent use in producing memorable stews? In fact no record of this form of killing has been found in the Home Circuit, and it could be construed that this is as good an example of the Law being an ass as one could expect to find.

In defence of 'Essex Man' it is worthwhile noting that a Steward of the second Earl called Arthur Wilson, who was present at some of the witch trials at Chelmsford over which the Earl presided, is quoted as declaring that:

> "...*(I) could see nothing in the evidence which did persuade me to think them other than poor, melancholy, envious, mischievous, ill-disposed, ill-dieted, atrabilious constitutions, whose fancies worked on gross fumes and vapours, might make the imagination ready to take any impression, and they themselves by the strength of fancy, may think they bring such things to pass which many times, unhappily they wish for and rejoice in when done, out of the malevolent humour which is in them; which passes with them as if they had really acted in it. And if there be an opinion in the people that such a body is a witch, their own fears (coming when they are) resulting from such dreadfull apprehension, do make every*

shadow an apparition; and every rat or cat an imp or spirit, which make so many tales and stories in the world, which have no shadow of truth."

Students of physics may care to note that Robert Boyle the chemist and physicist who was responsible for Boyle's Law, is on record as describing the buildings and land at Great Leez as 'delicious Leez' and that he was the brother of Mary Boyle, who when she was 15 years old, married the fourth (and last) Earl, Charles Rich. In 1753 the house and land at Great Leez were sold to Guys Hospital who, requiring only part of the house to serve as a farm house, demolished the remainder.

Details of Walk 2

Map required:
Ordnance Survey Pathfinder Map No 1098 (TL 61/71) Great and Little Waltham 1:25 000.
Starting and finishing point:
Great Leighs Priory
Grid reference TL 701 185.

The prescribed walk following the red arrows
Distance covered:
9.9 km (6.1 miles)
Duration of walk :
3 h 30 min. including a 30 minute break.
Condition of terrain:
Generally firm and relatively smooth.

The shorter walk following the green arrows
Distance covered:
5 km (3.1 miles)
Duration of walk:
2 h. including a 30 minute break.

Walking with our Heritage
Great and Little Leighs

Condition of terrain:
Generally firm and relatively smooth.

Place of Refreshment:
'The Compasses', public house at Littley Green.

The first part of both walks crosses the 'Pond Park' area which includes the old sites of the (now dried up) fish ponds. After passing Leighs Lodge the footpath leads down a made-up driveway to Lodge Lake, which is largely given over to private fishing. It then passes around the west end of the lake and continues for approximately 220 m (241 yd) along the south side of the lake, before turning due south to join the road.

It is at this point that the paths of the two sets of walkers diverge. Those opting for the shorter route should turn to the right and follow the road until they reach their original starting point at Leez Priory. Those who are following the prescribed walk should turn left and follow the road to Mattock's farm, where they should then turn right proceeding in a south easterly direction towards 'The Compasses' public house. Conveniently this part of the walk is about half way along the route and almost certainly it will be considered (by some), to be a suitable place for a break.

After the break the walk continues along the road through Littley Green for approximately 500 m (547 yd), when a signposted footpath will be seen on the right hand side, leading in a south westerly direction down towards a ford across the River Chelmer. For those who prefer to keep their feet dry a very slight diversion to the left of the main pathway will reveal a concrete footbridge.

The walk continues along a path with the name of 'Cut Throat Lane' which is, of course, tantalisingly graphic without in any way being self explanatory. A simple explanation for the derivation of the name could be that a local butcher operated in the area; however, local enquiries reveal that this particular stretch of road once linked the ford at Littley Green with another ford (also across the River

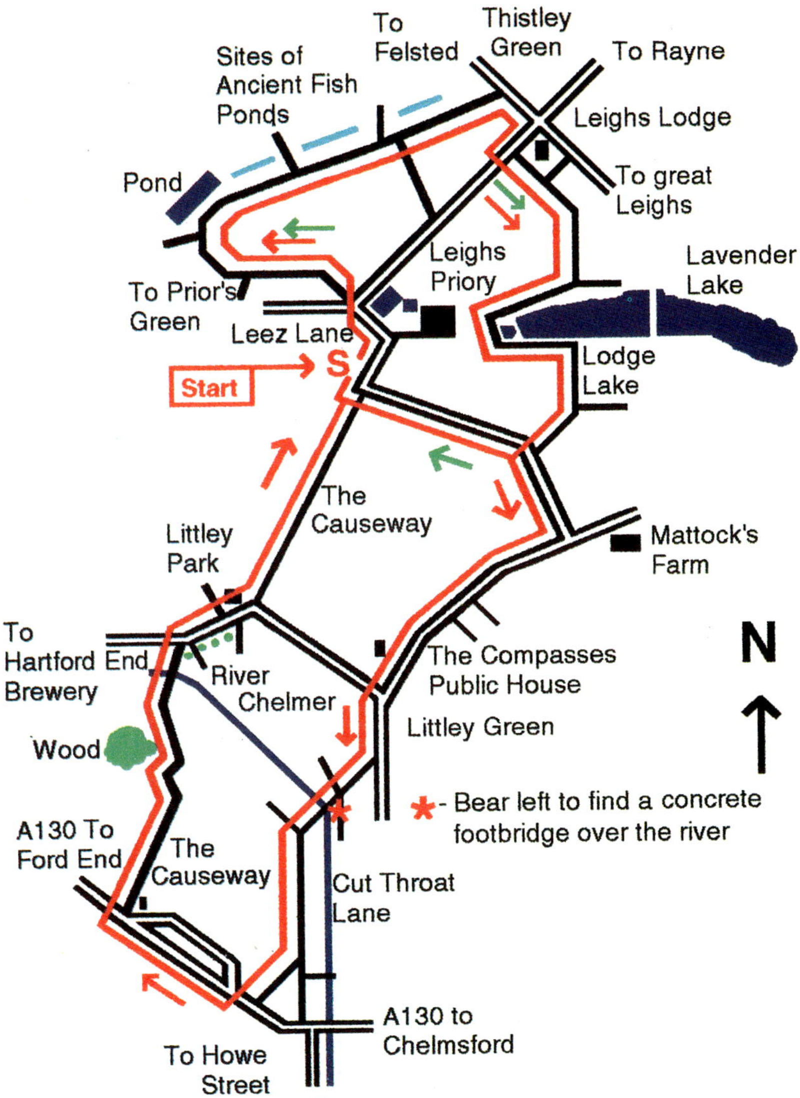

S - Starting point for both walks is from Great Leighs Priory, Grid Reference TL 701 185.
For the prescribed walk follow the red arrows.
For the shorter walk follow the green arrows.

Walk 2

● - Pollarded Elms

Chelmer), which was positioned north of the present new roadbridge over the A130. This ford was the last one to be found before entering Chelmsford, so guaranteeing that travellers could be expected to make use of Cut Throat Lane whenever they needed to cross the river. Such a situation would clearly have been of great assistance to potential thieves and it is tempting to conclude that the name of the road probably stemmed from this.

After joining the main A130 road walkers should turn right, travelling in a north westerly direction to a point just past the layby, when they should turn right into the bridleway which leads in a north easterly direction towards Hartford End. This bridleway is referred to as 'The Causeway' and it forms part of the approach into Leez Priory and what were once its Parks.

Soon after crossing the River Chelmer the bridleway joins a road which is lined with a number of old, dead pollarded elms. These and many more are shown on a map of the area drawn by Chapman and Andre in 1777 as marking the first section of 'The Causeway' leading through Littley Park towards the Priory. Such a feature would have made an impressive entrance and it is reasonable to conclude that they formed part of the original tree lined driveway dating from the time of Queen Elizabeth I. They are marked on the sketch map on that part of the walk just North of the river Chelmer crossing and, a pen and ink sketch of this part of the walk is also included.

During her visits to the Priory it is reasonable to suppose that the Queen's entourage would have used 'The Causeway' and in our case this forms the last part of the walk.

Pollarded Elms on The Causeway Hartford End

References

1 Nicholas C Lamming. 'A brief history of the buildings and people of Leez Priory Hartford End Essex' 3rd edition 1995.

2 A Victorian history of Essex Volume 2 p 155-156, Dewey classification no 942.67.

3 Information on witches was obtained from the Essex Record Office Library Dewey classification no 364.188 and also from the contents of box Z7.

4 Lloyd David (1635-1691), State Worthies I 920. The Essex Record Office Chelmsford.

Castle Hedingham

Walk 3

THE history of Castle Hedingham is extremely well documented and visits to the Castle and Church, together with a walk through the town are recommended.

Finds of stone and bronze implements show that the area was inhabited 2500 years ago and Roman pottery has been found on the school site in Church Lane. In Saxon times place names in Essex were sometimes made up by using the name of the local chief and combining it with the word 'ham', which meant a small settlement. Hence Hediningaham stood for 'the home of Hedin's people'. The modern spelling of Hedingham reflects the fact that over the centuries the spelling and sometimes the meaning of words in any living language are open to change.

Details of the Castle and its site

The early Britons living in the eastern parts of the country were often the victims of marauding bands from the Scandinavian countries across the North Sea and because of this, it became good practice when setting up a home, to choose a hilltop from which early warning of the approach of enemies could be assured. The mound on which the Hedingham fortification was eventually built was formed from a natural spur of land, all sides of which were then set to slopes. In Saxon times a wooden palisade would then have been erected around the perimeter of the mound in order to make the residents feel even more secure. Any enemy approaching from the north or east, would thus encounter earthworks and palisades, from the west

Hedingham Castle

impenetrable marshes and from the south a further palisaded ditch, which is referred to on a plan of the village of Castle Hedingham, prepared in 1592, as 'Dungyon Dytche' (see the sketch map where its route is now followed by a footpath). According to reference [1] part of this ditch may also have skirted the edge of a prison building.

Most Stately homes and Castles are expected to have an escape tunnel and Hedingham Castle is no exception. Edward Bingham in reference [2] refers somewhat circuitously in the following way to just such a tunnel.

> *"Somewhere near those steps to the 'Gardener's Cottage'[in Bayley Street]. I was told on good authority that about 1780 or so an arched entrance was found, and filled up again. This was the exit of a subterranean passage leading from the Castle, being (as was supposed) an outlet of escape for the garrison in time of siege."*

As a matter of interest reference [6] refers to a secret tunnel, recently discovered behind a wall and running in the direction of the village. A photograph is also given.

Some details of the de Vere family and their Legends

After William the Conqueror and his invading army of Normans defeated King Harold II at the battle of Hastings in 1066, he was subsequently crowned King of England and became known as William Ist.

Alberic (Albert) de Vere was a Norman who had sailed with William in 1066 and he is reputed to have come from the parish of Ver on the river Ver, below Coutances in the Cotentin in the La Manche in Normandy. He became a monk and founded Colne Priory where most of his descendants were subsequently buried. Of his descendants 20 were Earls and because of this the town became known as Earl's Colne. He died in 1088.

When Henry VIII carried out his 'Dissolution of the monasteries', the priory at Earl's Colne was destroyed. The surviving relatives of the de Vere family then removed the few remaining effigies to St. Stephen's Chapel (now restored) in Bures Suffolk, where they may still be seen.

An intriguing legend, centred around the de Vere family, concerns the origin of the name of the adjacent town of Royston. According to reference [1] Albert de Vere (the first Albert) married Beatrice, a half sister of William the Conqueror. A daughter of this marriage called Rohesia, is reputed to have had a cross mounted in a stone plinth set up on the way-side in North Hertfordshire, around which it is purported, a town subsequently developed called Rohesia's town, or as it is now known, Royston. The cross has not survived, but the stone plinth has and it may be seen at the junction of the A505 (the Icknield Way) and Royston High Street (the Ermine Way). It is now referred to by some of the local people as the 'Royse Stone'.

Interestingly, early historians have recognised that there is no shortage of candidature of ladies each having the name of Rohesia (Rosia or Rose), who could have been deemed important enough for such a legend to have arisen; so that there always has been a great deal of conjecture about the truth or otherwise of the legend. Inspection of a map of the area around Royston shows a large number of 'tumuli' and 'barrows', some of which date back to Neolithic times. Later, Danish invaders also set up sepulchres, by entombing their cremated dead; which method of burial was referred to as 'Royser' or 'at Royse' and, bearing in mind the large number of such sepulchres, it must be concluded that it is just as likely that the name of Royston may have originated from this practice, long before the Norman Conquest took place! The writer can understand why the past (and present) residents would not wish the name of their town to be associated with their cemetries and, in medieval times this may well have been the reasoning behind the need for an acceptable legend concerned with the naming of their town. For those readers who require further information on the naming of the town of Royston reference [5] covers the subject in more detail.

For his services during the campaign to conquer England Albert de Vere was given manors in Essex, Suffolk, Cambridgeshire and Middlesex. The land given in the latter County was referred to as 'Cheniston', it is now Kensington, which area does include a de Vere Gardens, in memory of the once prolific family of de Vere.

At the time of William the Conqueror, most European States operated on the feudal system and over a period of approximately six years, William introduced this system to England. In return for the giving of life grants of lands and offices to certain Lords, the King then required them in time of war or insurrection to support him by providing fighting men and suitable equipment. Over the centuries this arrangement produced such a proliferation of private armies, all with their own private livery, that the subsequent reigning Kings of England began to feel increasingly vulnerable as to possible 'takeovers'! Accordingly a law was passed which limited the number of liveried retainers which a man could command, to the number of his menial servants; this 'Statute of Liveries' led circa 1493, to a somewhat bruising experience for the 13th Earl of Oxford, John de Vere, Knight of the Garter.

John de Vere was 19 years old when during the reign of King Edward IV in 1461, his father and eldest brother were beheaded on Tower Hill. They espoused the Lancastrian cause in the War of the Roses, whereas the King was a Yorkist. Not surprisingly John de Vere himself became a staunch supporter of the Lancastrians and during his lifetime he helped to depose Edward IV and ultimately to ensure that the Earl of Richmond was crowned as Henry VII.

John de Vere entertained Henry lavishly at Castle Hedingham (date unknown), and, on leaving the Castle, the King walked the path to the Park gate (a distance of approximately 400 km), which was lined on both sides with de Vere's own liveried retainers:

> *"clothed in blue and costly apparel according to their several abilities, wearing the Earl's cognisance, and feathers in their hats."*

The Earl was aware of the 'Statute of Liveries' and must therefore have assumed that the King, having been entertained royally and knowing him to be a truly faithful subject, would be well enough disposed towards him to turn a 'blind eye' to such a blatant show of power. In fact Henry took the opposite view and according to reference [1], when the King came to the end of the walk, he turned about and called the Earl to him, and said;

> *"My Lord I have heard much of your hospitality, but I see it is greater than is spoken. These handsome gentlemen and yeomen whom I see on both sides of me are sure your menial servants."*

At which the Earl smiled and said:

> *"It may please your Grace that were not for mine ease; they are most of them my retainers, and come to do me service at such a time as this, and chiefly to see your Grace."*

Whereat the King startled a little, and said:

> *"By my faith, my Lord, I thank you for my good cheer, but I may not endure to have my laws broken in my sight: my attorney must speak with you about it."*

In the fullness of time the Attorney General spoke and de Vere found himself having to pay a fine of 15,000 marks, which the Reverend Severne Ashurst Majendie estimated to be worth £10,000 in the English money of that time and which in 1904 was considered to be equivalent to £100,000. If the average rate of inflation per year since 1904 is taken to be 2% then over 100 years £100,000 at compound interest becomes approximately £725,000 and at 3% average inflation per year, becomes approximately £2,000,000! Clearly King Henry VII did not hesitate to make an example of one of his richest and most faithful supporters, which action certainly made him appear to be altogether ruthless, covetous and very insecure.

The title of Earl of Oxford was first given by the Empress Matilda (later confirmed by her son Henry II), to Aubery the third. He was a Crusader and according to reference [1], due to a series of deliberate mistranslations of his name, based on his adoption of a boar having a stern or grim appearance, as a badge, became known as 'Grymme Aubery' de Vere. Stonemasons are well known for their propensity to indulge in 'little jokes' and those who visit the church will be able to see the first Earls reputed (grim) likeness, carved in stone and set in the corner of the south facing wall. It must be recorded however that there is a school of thought which maintains that the stone likeness is in fact that of one of the mother superiors of the church and, examination of the pen and ink sketch of the image does seem to reveal a certain curvaceousness in the lines of the face.

Details of some of the occupants of Kirby Hall

Kirby Hall is included in the walk and it was originally home to a Richard Kirkby and his successors, who lived there from 1256 to 1360. The house and estate were then subsequently owned by three other different families, until 1468 when a John Kirkby again took possession, before selling out to the family of de Vere.

'Grymme Aubery' - Castle Hedingham Church

In circa 1580 John de Vere commenced living at Kirby Hall where he made a home for his mother, three brothers and a sister. These brothers became known as the 'fighting Veres'. They were Francis de Vere, Horace Lord Vere of Tilbury Manor, (an estate just North of Castle Hedingham) and Robert de Vere. In fact many other de Veres could be included under the banner of the 'fighting Veres'. To illustrate this a quote from page 65 of reference [1] which refers to the time of the wars of the Netherlands is as follows:

> *"The noble house of Vere had certainly not spared its blood. Lord (Horace) Vere's own brother Robert, heads the list of slain; next, the eighteenth Earl of Oxford fell at Breda, Sir Edward Vere at Bois-le-Duc, the nineteenth Earl and young Edward Vere at Maastricht, while Francis and Horace were riddled with wounds."*

Both Francis and later Horace were buried in Westminster Abbey.

An overall appreciation of the life and times of the Earls of Oxford can be found in reference [3] (which can be obtained from the castle bookshop) and, detailed accounts of the exploits of the de Veres are given in reference [1].

A quote from a poem by Thomas Gray (1716-71) who (unlike most of the de Veres), spent a large part of his life in scholarly pursuits, might provide a salutary end to our thoughts on deeds of daring:

> *"Can storied urn or animated bust*
> *Back to its mansion call the fleeting breath?*
> *Can Honour's voice provoke the silent dust?*
> *Or flatt'ry soothe the dull cold fear of death?"*

Details of Walk 3

Map required:
Ordnance Survey Pathfinder Map No 1051 (TL 63/73)
Thaxted and Sible Hedingham 1:25 000.
Starting and finishing point:
Junction of the A604 with Nunnery Street Castle Hedingham.
Grid reference TL 777 355.

The prescribed walk following the red arrows.
Distance covered:
8.4 km (5.2 miles)
Duration of walk:
3 hours. including a 30 minute break.
Condition of terrain:
Generally firm and relatively smooth.

The shorter walk following the green arrows.
Distance covered:
5.2 km (3.2 miles)
Duration of walk:
2 hours including a 30 minute break.
Condition of terrain:
Generally firm and relatively smooth.

Places of Refreshment:
A wide selection of places are available in Castle Hedingham.

The walks commence at Crouch Green on which for many years in the month of May, the Great Fairs of Castle Hedingham were held. The hill on the main road nearby was known as 'Cow Fair Hill', where predictably, cattle were bought and sold. Another annual fair took place in July, when the venue was centred in St. James's Street. Sadly, similar occasions no longer take place. In those times, according to Edward Bingham, writing in the Parish magazine of 1895 reference [2], it was possible to obtain a licence to sell beer from one's house or cottage for a period

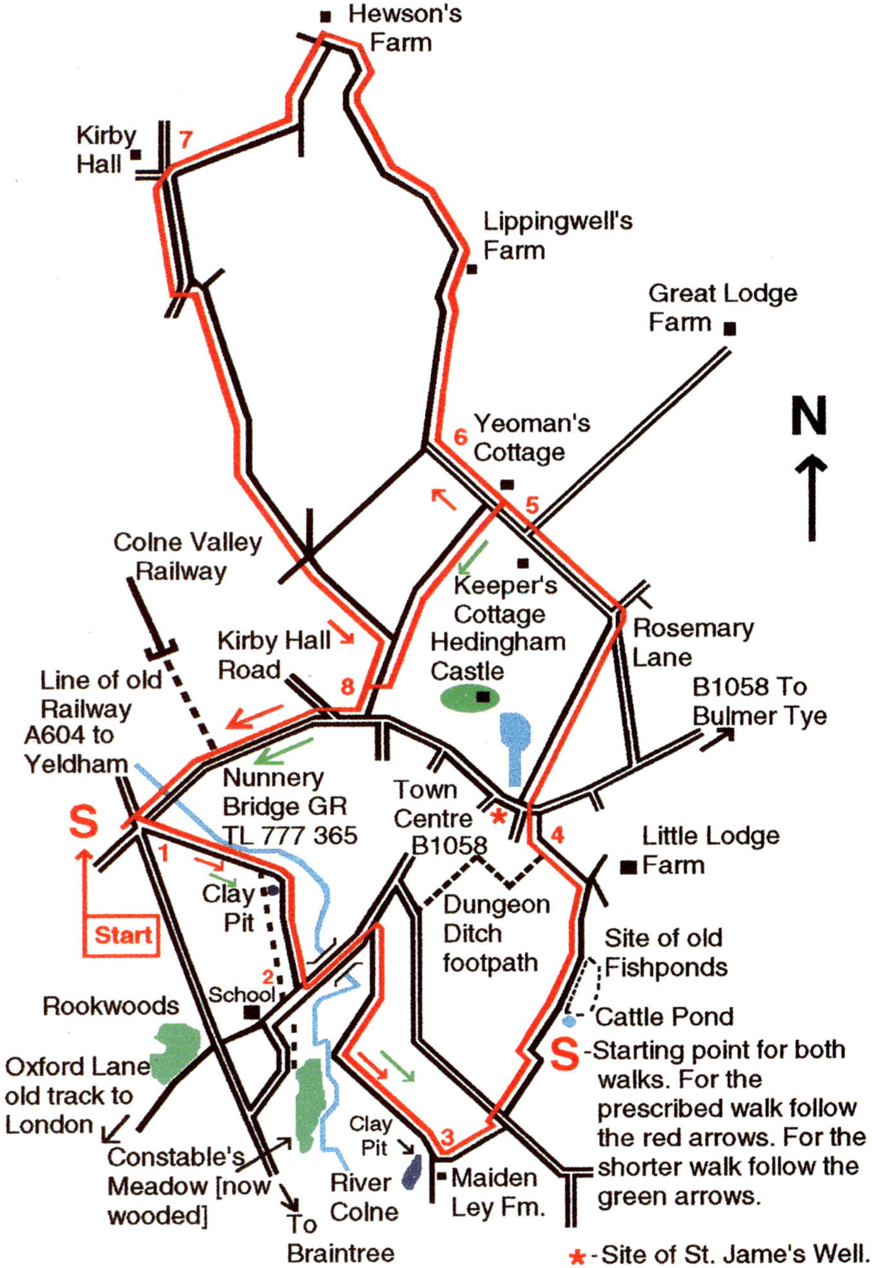

Hewson's Farm
Kirby Hall
7
Lippingwell's Farm
Great Lodge Farm
N
Yeoman's Cottage
6
5
Colne Valley Railway
Keeper's Cottage
Hedingham Castle
Rosemary Lane
Kirby Hall Road
8
Line of old Railway
B1058 To Bulmer Tye
A604 to Yeldham
Nunnery Bridge GR TL 777 365
Town Centre B1058
S
4
Little Lodge Farm
1
Clay Pit
Start
Dungeon Ditch footpath
Site of old Fishponds
2
School
Rookwoods
Cattle Pond
S -Starting point for both walks. For the prescribed walk follow the red arrows. For the shorter walk follow the green arrows.
Oxford Lane old track to London
Clay Pit
3
Constable's Meadow [now wooded]
Maiden Ley Fm.
River Colne
To Braintree
* -Site of St. Jame's Well.

Walk 3

covering the duration of a fair. A log of wood was then placed in front of the house to provide a convenient seat while the liquor was being consumed and such establishments became known as 'bough houses'. Bingham goes on to record:

> *"Vice and profligacy were rampant there, under the shelter of the 'bough,' and the scenes outside were sufficient indications of the orgies within."*

He goes on to write:

> *"Later on in our own day (1895) the once useful fair became a thing of the past, and so noted for being the great rendevous of vice, drunkenness, and immorality that the Lord of the Manor abolished both it and St. James's fair."*

So there!

The part of the walk from 1 to 2 on the sketch map, follows the route of the river Colne and crosses over the site of a Benedictine Nunnery, which was founded circa 1190 by the Countess Lucia De Vere, the third wife of Aubrey De Vere (the third), who had in 1142 become the first of 20 Earls of Oxford. Nothing of the original form of the Priory buildings can now be seen on the surface. The countess became the first Prioress and according to reference [1], 'was much mourned on her demise'.

On the west side of the footpath is a small clay pit which in common with many similar pits in the area was used to provide material for the process of 'wattle and daub', then used to line the walls of dwelling places. The surrounding area has been planted with willow trees and is designated as a meadow under the auspices of the Countryside Commission.

At point 2 on the sketch map where the footpath crosses the B1058 road, readers may be interested to know that according to reference [2], the old road to London from Castle Hedingham was merely a track and lay in a south westerly direction past the present school, across the Yeldham road and past Rookwoods, at which point it was referred to as Oxford Lane.

The map associated with the survey of Castle Hedingham carried out in 1592 shows that two acres of land (now wooded), lying SW of the river between points 2 and 3, was designated for use by the Constable of the castle as a meadow.

Between points 3 and 4 of the walk is Little Lodge farm. The farmhouse was built in 1588 by the 17th Earl and was used by him and his family and friends, as a convenient place to stay when engaged in falconry and deer hunting in the surrounding forests. The Lodge was later let to John De Vere a cousin of the 17th Earl for use as a farmhouse. South of the farmhouse the footpath passes around a cattle pond (referred to as a reservoir on the Pathfinder map) and this, according to reference [2] 'is the only remains of two shallow fish ponds of some acres in extent which were used for fattening fish for the Earl's table'. The rough outlines of these ponds are within an area which is now under the Stewardship of the Countryside Commission and can be seen on the east side of the footpath. Although not mentioned by Bingham, one may conjecture that the fish ponds would also have offered a satisfactory source of sustenance for the local poachers!

At point 4 on the sketch map the survey map of 1592 shows the present road to Sudbury (the B1058), as consisting of a 'pathway' starting from the junction of St James's Street and Bayley Street and following the footpath shown on the sketch map from point 4 in a NE direction. The old site of St James's well is adjacent to the present small brick built pumping station. For many years residents drew their water from a pump at the site, but this has now gone. The water that once filled the well is now channelled into an underground concrete chamber and at one time was used to supply the village. However subsequent building development made this unrealistic. The water can be seen flowing underground, by looking down into a standard surface water collection drain, sited in the roadway at the kerb, just a few paces down the hill towards the village. The Reverend Severne Ashurst Majendie describes the waters of the well in reference [1] as being 'ferruginous' and in the time of Lady Lucia they were believed to have healing properties.

Points 5 and 6 on the sketch map mark the start of the two routes to all points North of the castle. At least two routes would have been in use so that in times of bad weather, the messengers and other travellers would nearly always be able to find a viable route in the general direction of their journey.

The footpath heading north east of point 5 leads to another old house at Great Lodge farm, which according to reference [2] is of an earlier date than that at Little Lodge and it also, was used as a base from which to hunt. The Northern route from the castle continues from point 6 to Hewson's Farm where a track leads in a south easterly direction towards Kirby Hall at point 7 on the sketch map.

At point 8 on the sketch map the footpath joins Nunnery Street which leads back to the starting point of the walk.

References

1 Majendie, Severne A. Ashurst (Rev). Some account of the family of De Vere, the Earls of Oxford, and of Hedingham Castle in Essex Nov 1904.

2 Bingham Edward. Castle Hedingham in the Olden Times. Castle Hedingham Church magazine Feb. 1895.

3 Innes-Smith Robert. The Earls of Oxford. Reprinted from 'East Anglian Life'.

4 Brochure dealing with Castle Hedingham Open Village and Flower Festival 24-25 June 1967. Available in The Chelmsford Record Office.

5 Kingston Alfred. A History of Royston, published by Warren Bros. and Cooke Ltd., Upper King Street Royston, Herts. SG8 9ZF.

6 Bird Charles James. Historic Castle Hedingham. Available from the Castle bookshop.

Thaxted

Walk 4

THE town is situated between Dunmow and Radwinter, on the B184, parts of which follow the route of a Roman road. Roman coins, ornaments and bricks have been found at 'Claypits' south east of the town and at Clarance House in Watling Street.

As a Saxon settlement it has been credited with various names and reference [1], quoting from an unstated 'authority', gives 'Thaegenestede', subsequently contracted to 'Thaegestede'. The same source goes on to explain – *"that 'Thaegen' means 'Thane' and therefore 'Thaegenestede' would mean the place or town of a Thane".* In the Domesday book (1086) the town is referred to as 'Thane land' and is shown on the Domesday map as 'Tachesteda', [2]. The Reverend Symonds goes on to suggest that as the Normans were not used to sounding 'th' they softened it to a 't' and that on deeds drawn up during the time of their influence, the town is also referred to as 'Tastede' and 'Tacstede' and towards the end of the reign of Edward I (1272-1307) as 'Taxstede', which latter name is very close to the pleasingly shorter present name of 'Thaxted'.

On the other hand, reference [3] states that the place name is derived from two Old English words 'thaec', from which the material used for thatching takes its name and 'sted', a place. Hence the combination of the words 'Thaecsted', signify 'a place where reeds or other plants used in thatching grow'.

This author would like to suggest that both the above derivations could be correct; with the Old English version 'Thaecsted' being used circa 407-1000 AD, as developed by the Anglo-Saxons; and with the Middle English version

'Taxstede' being used circa 1066-1500 as developed by the Normans. Its present name 'Thaxted', the (Modern English version), being used circa 1500 to the present day.

John Betjeman expressed the following sentiments about Thaxted:

> *'There is no town in North Essex - and very few in England to equal in beauty, compactness and juxtaposition of medieval and Georgian architecture the town of Thaxted.'*

The Norman Conquest took place in 1066 and it took about six years for William to establish the Manorial System in England. This involved transferring the ownership of land and buildings to new owners who (predictably), were Normans. In the case of Thaxted the dispossessed owner was a Saxon Thane called 'Eluric' and, the (no doubt) grateful new owner was Richard, son of Gilbert the Earl of Brion (one of William's relations). The ownership of the Manor of Thaxted has, since that time, often been in the hands of individuals who were closely associated with Royalty. At one time it was owned by Elizabeth, daughter of Edward IV who subsequently became the Queen of Henry VII. Later Henry VIII made the Manor over to Catherine of Arragon who then leased it to Sir John Cutte who was Treasurer of the Household to King Henry VIII.

Thaxted is first referred to as a Borough in 1334 and the town was at its most prosperous during the reign of Edward III (1327-77), when according to reference[4] approximately one third of the population were Cutlers. Stan Jarvis in reference[5] suggests that the trade began in the 12th century and continued for 400 years, this being the length of time required for the indigenous supply of wood to become exhausted.

Compared with traditional blacksmith's work, the forging of cutlery is a relatively delicate process requiring less heat, so that the use of wood as a fuel, combined with forced air from a bellows, was probably sufficient for their purposes. The local use of charcoal would probably have been reserved for the working of heavier ironmongery.

The Cutlers of the town formed a Guild and later built the Guildhall in Town Street, which was used as a gathering place for local tradesmen. Cutler's Green is to be found to the west of the town on the Debden Road and it was at this place that some of the forges were situated. Forges were also to be found in Bull-ford Street (now Bolford Street). Much later in 1881, sparks from a blacksmith's forge in this street started a fire which subsequently damaged much of the town and details of this including an 'eye witness account', are given in reference[6].

Following the decline in the manufacture of cutlery, the prosperity of the town had to rely solely on the efforts of the agricultural workers and, in 1583 in an attempt to enhance the finances of the town, some Flemish and French Huguenot refugee clothiers and fustian weavers were introduced; a Guild of clothiers was established and they practised their trade for about 50 or so years and then left. Notwithstanding this, Thaxted in common with many other towns in Essex had a considerable woollen weaving industry, which flourished from the 16th to the 18th centuries. However, in spite of the combined efforts of the trades-people and the agricultural workers, the town's finances languished once more, to such an extent that in 1685 James II was instrumental in making the town give up its Charter as a Borough.

Visitors to the town will no doubt discover that a house in Fishmarket Street (adjacent to the Guildhall), is referred to as 'Dick Turpin's Cottage'. Others believe that the house belonged to his uncle (a butcher), with whom Dick Turpin (the notorious highwayman), is said to have stayed from time to time. In Turpin's younger days he was apprenticed to a butcher in Whitechapel, but was dismissed for bad behaviour; so it is possible that he took up butchery in his uncle's house, perhaps during those periods when he wished to avoid the Law.

Stoney Lane was once the original highway through the town. The lane joins on to a path across the churchyard which joins up with Newbiggen Street, which was a Roman road, known in the 14th century as 'Vikere Street'. It is interesting to note that in many medieval towns traveller's steps were routed across the entrance to the local church, which establishment assumed a very much greater role in the life of the community than is at present the case.

According to reference [6], Gustav Holst lived in a thatched cottage in Monk Street from 1914-25 where he composed 'The Planets' and the hymn which has the opening line:

'I vow to thee my Country, all earthly things above,'

He also took part in the musical life of the Church and a plaque unveiled in 1961 by Sir Adrian Boult, is fixed on the wall of his 'music room', next door to 'The Manse' in Town Street.

A well known charity in the town which has been in existence since approximately 1490, is 'Yardley's charity'. This came into being when Thomas Yerdele died without male issue in 1443 and in his Will he stipulated that the income from his estate should subsequently be devoted to the repair of the church, the highways of Thaxted and the relief of the poorest inhabitants. Yardley's moated farm and hall were mentioned in the Domesday Book and they are situated approximately 2.8 km (1.75 miles), north west of the town. The Yardley Trustees still minister to local needs.

Another charity is one referred to as 'the Queen's Cloth'. This took the form of a gift by Henry VIII (at the instigation of his then Queen), in the sum of £6 to provide clothing for the most indigent and aged people of the parish. The interest from this bequest is now miniscule and Mark Arman (writing in 1995), notes that the last gift was in the early 1970s!

In 1911, Morris dancing was revived in Thaxted due to the efforts of the 'rebel priest', Father Conrad Noel and following upon the efforts of many other interested parties,

The Guildhall - Thaxted

The Windmill - Thaxted

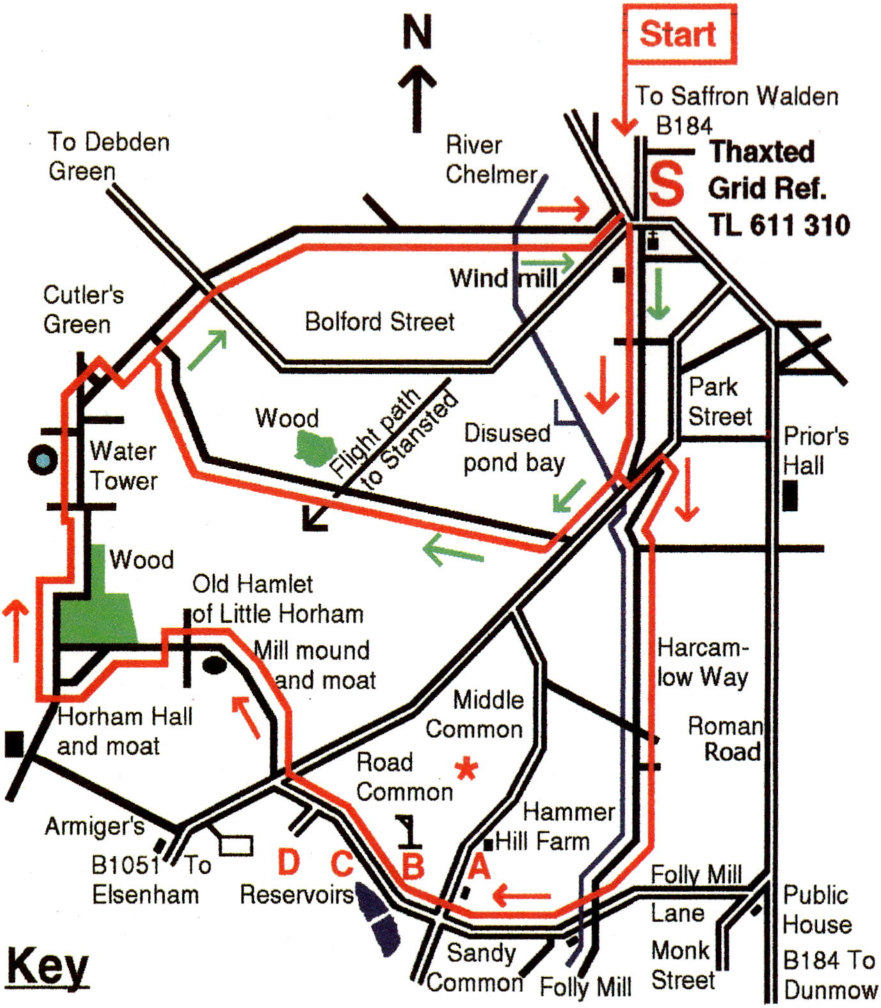

Key

A - Old site of two Blackdeath cottages
B - Gibbet crossroads
C - Possible site for a picnic
D - Disused gravel pit
***** - All commons are now farmed.

S - Starting point for both walks.
For the prescribed walk
follow the red arrows.
For the shorter walk
follow the green arrows.

Walk 4

Thaxted has now become a National Centre for the practice and advancement of the tradition of Morris dancing. A portrait of Father Noel is hung in the Guildhall but sadly he is not wearing his Morris costume!

The Church of St. John the Baptist

The church is built upon a hill in the centre of the town, making it the most prominent building in the area. It was built, as so many other churches were, on the site of previous churches and it is likely that the present building was started circa 1315, by the combined efforts of the local tradesmen and the son of Elizabeth De Clare, the Earl of Ulster. The work was continued circa 1377 by Edmund Mortimer, Earl of March and Ulster and later on by Edward IV, who is known to have arranged for building to be done around 1465 and also at a later period.

There is a superbly succinct memorial in the church to an early 19th century builder called Peter Platt, who took on the job of restoring the church tower. It reads:

"Where Peter lies, 'tis fit this tower should show But for his skill, itself had lain as low."

A tiny chapel on the west side of the main entrance to the church is dedicated to a priest from Colchester, the Blessed John Ball, who for his sympathies with the cause of the rebels during the Peasants' Revolt in 1381 was thrown into jail. He was later released by the Kentish peasants, subsequently leading them in their confrontations with Richard II over the Manorial system. At Mile End in London the King granted the peasants various worthless 'Charters of Rights', after which they were persuaded to return home. Later however, Richard led an army into Essex and, at Waltham, informed a deputation of rebels that:

"Villeins you are; in bondage you shall abide,

and that not your old bondage, but one incomparably worse".

Later the Manorial Rolls of the Manor of Thaxted were destroyed and the Manor House was demolished. Happily for all our agricultural workers, subsequent events did not turn out as the King intended!

During the Civil War of 1645 Thaxted Church (in common with many other churches in the area) was desecrated, the windows were broken and the building was used to stable horses.

Details of Walk 4

Map required:
Ordnance Survey Pathfinder Maps Nos. 1051 (TL 63/73) Thaxted and Sible Hedingham 1:25 000 and, 1075, 1074 and 1050.
Starting and finishing point:
Thaxted Church
Grid reference TL 611 310.

The prescribed walk following the red arrows
Distance covered:
8.1 km (5.0 miles).
Duration of walk:
3 hours. including a 30 minute break.
Condition of terrain:
Generally firm and relatively smooth.

The shorter walk following the green arrows
Distance covered:
4.0 km (2.5 miles).
Duration of walk:
1 h 45 min. including a 30 minute break
Condition of terrain:
Generally firm and relatively smooth.

Places of Refreshment:
The town of Thaxted has many tea rooms, restaurants and public houses.
The Farmhouse Inn and Restaurant which is situated in Monk Street 365 m (400 yd) due East of Folly Mill.

Both walks start from the Bull Ring and take place along part of the Harcamlow Way, which delineates approximately 225km (140 miles) of footpaths, following the 'low' route from Harlow to Cambridge. The windmill shown on the sketch map originally belonged to John Webb. It was built in 1804 on the site of an earlier mill, which reference [7] refers to as 'Chirchemylle'. Medieval accounts show that this first mill was repaired in 1377, but by 1770 it had disappeared. The lower floors of the present mill, house a rural museum and the upper floors contain the mill mechanism, now mostly restored.
The building is owned by the Parish Council and the restoration was carried out using grants obtained from the Department of the Environment, the County Council and Yardley's Charity.

The land between Park Street to the east of the footpath is called 'Manor Gardens', to the west, extending as far as Cutler's Green, was 'Little Park'. Thaxted contained three large parks, which in the Middle Ages were regarded as status symbols and it was necessary to obtain a licence from the Crown to 'impark'. This meant that each park was surrounded by palings so that deer for hunting and the table, could be contained within the enclosed areas. All the parks were well wooded and the coppice underwood was a source of fuel for the cutlers.

To the west of the footpath and extending across the flood plain of the river is a disused pond bay, which is now concealed from view behind some pine trees in a wood. The path of the river has been re-routed to by-pass the ancient dam, which was once the site of a watermill recorded in the Domesday Book. Originally the dam would have contained the water from the River Chelmer, forming a mill pond reaching as far back as the road to Cutler's Green and, it is thought that at some time the pond may also have been used by the local cloth industry for whitening and removing grease from fleeces, a process referred to as 'fulling'.

The house now known as Folly Mill, is referred to by Chapman and Andre on their map of 1776 as 'Foley', which it is believed was meant at that time to indicate that it was situated in a leafy area, which happily is still true today. The old site of Sandy Common (the first of three Commons), lies south of Folly Mill Lane on ground which is now called 'The Stepps'. The sites of the two other pieces of Common ground were north of Folly Mill Lane. These were called 'Road Common' and 'Middle Common' and they are marked on the Ordnance Survey map of 1876-7, but currently they appear to have been 'absorbed' into the surrounding farm land.

Next we come to Gibbet's Cross, which is a good example of 'sunken crossroads'. In early times road surfaces were unmetalled, so that whenever a hill was negotiated the combined effects of footsteps, horse's hooves, wagon wheels, and rain and frost, was to lower the road surface relative to the surrounding area. The gibbet was erected high above the road on land which formed part of Middle Common, immediately adjacent to the western side of the road running north towards Thaxted (see sketch map). Clearly the site was chosen so that any recipient of such punishment would be visible from all directions and would therefore be seen by as many citizens as possible. As it was the custom to make felons transport themselves to their place of execution, it is likely that they would have taken their first walk of the morning (and the last walk of their lives), from the Town's jail to this spot; having travelled approximately the same distance as that covered on the first part of this walk.

In the 14th century, at the time of the Black Death, it was thought necessary to isolate those who were suffering from the disease, so that Thaxted had a 'Pest House' north of the town. According to local tradition it also had two cottages sited adjacent to Gibbet Cross (see sketch map); these were subsequently burnt down, but their position is shown on the Ordnance Survey map of 1876-7.

A possible site for a break is indicated on the sketch map, which now offers a relaxing view of two reservoirs. It is a salutary thought that from this position it would at one time have just been possible to catch a glimpse of the latest candidate for the gallows!

On crossing the B1051 road from Thaxted to Elsenham the walk uses a bridleway, which leads to the hamlet of Little Horeham, shown on the map of 1776 by Chapman and Andre. The same hamlet is shown on the Ordnance Survey map of 1876-7, as being 'Little Horham' situated in Little Horham Lane. However the 'Lane' has today become the bridleway and Little Horham has disappeared and it is no longer shown on current maps. A moat and the mound upon which a post mill was once sited lies in the area which is now wooded.

The next part of the walk takes in Horham Hall (spelt Horeham by Chapman and Andre and others before 1776) The first development of the site took place around 1470 by Robert Large, a Lord Mayor of London. However these buildings were nearly all pulled down by Sir John Cutte in the early part of the 16th century, when he built a larger house on the same site. Part of Cutte's house has itself been taken down, but that which remains is a fine example of Tudor construction. It is interesting to note that currently the border between the parishes of Broxted and Thaxted passes through the kitchen of the House and that according to information given in reference [8], the name of the Hall was derived from the Saxon 'ora' a skirt or border and, 'ham' a place.

As the footpath approaches Horham Hall it crosses the grand drive from Armigers to the entrance of the Hall a distance of 800 m (0.5 mile) and it is along this route that Queen Elizabeth I came as a guest of John Cutte the second, with all her carriages and approximately 300 baggage carts, to stay at the Hall in 1571 for nine days and, in 1578 for five days.

On the last occasion she had the satisfaction of scotching a marriage proposal, which appears to have been first put forward about two years previously, on behalf of the Duke of Anjou, a brother of the King of France. The Duke did not appear in person but sent an envoy on his behalf, a Monsieur Baguebille. The following extracts are taken from 'Queen Elizabeth at Horeham, The Calendar of State Papers 1578-79' in which Lord Burghley reported on what took place at the meeting:

> *"Her Majesty said she could not but thank the Duke, his master, for his goodwill in sending to renew the suit of marriage, tho' it had been intermitted almost two years. For his reason alleged to excuse this, as in no wise proceeding from himself, she said she was content to admit some, but others she could not allow of. As for the matter itself concerning her marriage with anyone she continued in the mind wherein she had always been firmly determined and had so answered no small number of princes, that she would never marry anyone whom she should not first herself see."*

The rest of the account as transcribed by Lord Burghley indicates that the Queen was also well aware of the personal and political consequences which could arise from such a meeting as the next extract shows:

> *"....but if it (a subsequent meeting) should not succeed as he (the Duke) desires, he would not alter his goodwill; but that the friendship professed not only between his brother (the King of France) and her but between the Duke and her might continue without diminution.--- She added that this manner of dealing was only what had*

passed from her to a number of princes in like case, as to the Emperor Maximilian, for his brother, the King of Sweden and others."

The reader will not be surprised to learn that the proposed meeting did not take place!

The walk now doubles back on itself for a short distance skirting the western boundary of Home Wood before returning to Thaxted via Cutler's Green.

References

1 Symonds the Rev. George E. 'Thaxted and its Cutler's Guild'. Transactions of the Essex Archaeological Society 1889 New Series III pp 255-61.

2 Powell Raymond W. Essex In Domesday Book, Essex Record Office publication 1990.

3 Thaxted in Essex, a short guide to the buildings of historical and architectural interest, 1951. Essex Record Office box T1 (B).

4 Insall D.W. and Associates. Chartered Architects and Planning Consultants. Town Planning Report - Thaxted an Historical and Architectural Survey for the County Council of Essex, 1966.

5 Jarvis Stan. Essex a County History, Countryside Books, Newbury, Berkshire.

6 Arman Mark. A short Historical Guide to the Ancient Town of Thaxted, 1980 2nd edit. Essex Record Office Box T1 (B).

7 Hunter John M. Historic features of the Thaxted Landscape. The Thaxted bulletin, (1) Spring(41) 1988,(2) Autumn (42) 1988.

8 Visit to Horham Hall and the Thaxted District, Sat. July 1st 1933 printed in the Essex Naturalist, Vol XXIV, pp.157-161.

Newport

Walk 5 – West of Newport

THE name of Newport was given to an existing settlement north east of Bonhunt; when it was designated both as a 'new' Royal Market Town and a tax collecting centre for the 'Hundred of Uttles Ford'. This is believed to have occurred during the reign of King Edward the Elder (899-924), who was the son of Alfred the Great. In late Saxon times Newport was one of 10 royal market towns in Essex and it was the only such town in the north west of the County. Its details were later recorded in the Domesday Book where it is listed as 'Neuport'. The manor of Newport was at one time held by Earl Harold, who when he became King Harold (the last Anglo-Saxon King of England), was destined to lose the battle of Hastings (and his life), to the Normans in 1066.

In the 10th century, in order to increase revenue and to try and limit the sale of stolen goods, the Saxon kings granted market licences. These licenced outlets for goods were referred to as 'ports' and according to Bernard Nurse [1], Edward the Elder made regulations designed to restrict the exchange of goods to these designated 'ports'. (Readers will be aware that it is not unknown nowadays for car-boot sales to provide outlets for stolen property). Market charters for Newport continued to be granted and renewed by the Norman kings and by King John, at various times from 1227 to 1472 and such markets continued until the late 19th century, when they were known locally as 'Colt Fairs'.

From around the time of the Norman invasion and until the late 18th century, many of the inhabitants of Newport obtained their income from the production and weaving of wool. Also from the mid 14th to the late 18th century, saffron crocus bulbs were grown in the region and the stigmas of the flowers were then used as a colouring for foods and liqueurs, as a dye for fabrics and as a flavouring for food. In the first part of the 18th century, much income was obtained from servicing the needs of travellers from London to Newmarket and at this time Newport contained a total of 10 inns.

Like all other towns Newport was responsible for the 'treatment' of its own poor. Their needs were dealt with by a body of people referred to as the 'Vestry' and they were given the power to set and levy a local rate to finance the cost of providing a Workhouse. The Vestry Book for the period from 1706 to 1844 was discovered in 1990 and it has yielded an enormous amount of information on the manner in which these responsibilities were discharged. Any potential entrant to the workhouse would obviously have to obey the rules of the establishment and the following extract would no doubt have been sufficient to convince any person that perhaps he or she should explore alternative arrangements!

Extract Joy Pugh [1]:

> *"....3 That everyone perform their stint as the master or vestry or chosen men shall appoint or to be chastized for their idleness or shortened in their diet besides and what they do above their stint is for their own encouragement. If any abuse their work, to the House of Correction for the slash. The overplus of the young will help to supply ye defect of ye old.*
>
> *4 That they be present at 6 in the morning till 7 at night in the Summer time; at other seasons as shall be appointed. Their absence without leave to be chastized.*
>
> *5 Their diet to be bread and cheese, milk or broth at 9 in the morning and 7 at night and*

meat at one of ye clock at noon, or on Sunday meat and pudding; Monday ye relics and meat broth, Tuesday pease and pork and beans, Wednesday pease pottage or dumplins, Thursday meat, Friday fishe, Saturday dumpling......

....8 A warrant to be always in hand for ye immediate correction of those who anyways transgress or disobey their orders or do not perform ye stint. Item yt ye poor people themselves personally appear monthly at ye vestry before ye townsmen if they may seek clothes and apparel to be decent or to see if they can answer any complaint.

9 Swearing, lying, stealing, obscene discourse, neglect of the Lord's Day is to be immediately punished with severity."

The use of church bells and handbells.

According to Dr D I Gordon [2], from the time of the Norman conquest to 1875, a wakening and a curfew bell were rung daily from the church tower at 4.00 am and at 8.00 pm. This was necessary because clocks were not generally owned by the local populace. Also up to 1914 a bell was rung each weekday at 7.57 am and at 8.03 pm, the number of rings signifying the day of the month. Again at 9.00 am, a large or small bell was rung on the day after the demise of an adult or of a child.

On Christmas day the village bellman could be heard crying as follows:

"Rise, maids, arise,
Heat your ovens and bake your pies,
Don't forget to hang on your pots,

And see the old bellman ain't forgot.
[variable].
It is now half past four o'clock on a cold and frosty morning."

The bellmen were allowed to collect for themselves on Oak Apple Day and on Plough Monday. On Oak Apple Day a bough would be placed against each front door, so that when the door was opened it would fall into the opening, providing a not too subtle hint that largesse was required for their services. Also on Plough Monday, non subscribers ran the risk of having part of their front path ploughed up.

Saint Mary's Church Newport

It is not known whether a Saxon church existed on the same site as the present church. However some astute reasoning on the part of Dr D I Gordon [2], (paraphrased below) suggests that at the time of the Normans a Saxon church may have existed there.

Traditionally those who built castles could be relied upon to choose a commanding site, but in the case of Newport even though the elevation of the land was lower than that occupied by the church, it is supposed that the Normans built a castle on the mound where the Grammar school is now situated. Both sites had natural water supplies, so that this would not have been a reason for the Grammar school site being chosen and the implication is that an important building, perhaps a Saxon church, was already occupying the higher ground. Interestingly it is now considered by reference[3] to be equivocal that the Grammar School site ever encompassed a castle and this reference refers to a nearby deviation in the old Walden Road as circumnavigating a 'substantial obstacle, possibly the castle'.

During the Middle Ages it became fashionable for wealthy individuals to leave land, money, and property to the Church, in order that regular masses could be said for the benefit of the souls of the donor and his family. Coincidentally, the Church Establishment also had a rule forbidding the celebration of mass more than once per day at any one altar [4]. Predictably, during the affluent years, the continued receipt of bequests for the saying of mass, quickly reached saturation point, requiring that the church should be enlarged and furnished with more altars! When such a stratagem was also linked to the receiving of property, the owning of which was deemed to be unworthy (unless it was held by Churchmen), it becomes clear that the efforts of these erstwhile men of God at 'empire building' were second to none.

Just prior to 1000 AD, there was a widely held belief that the Day of Judgement would coincide with the coming of the first millennium and when it did not, this resulted in a spate of church renovations and rebuilding, ostensibly carried out as acts of thanksgiving. Substantial rebuilding of the church at Newport using flint, pebbles and limestone, took place a little later around 1220 to 1240 [2]. The church roof at that time was low and sharply pitched and the outline can be seen today on the exterior of the East wall.

More building took place throughout the 14th, 15th and 16th centuries, finally resulting in a church whose size was a reflection of the relative prosperity of those times, but which was considered by some to be large for the size of the Parish. The same can also be said to be true of many other churches; in particular the church at Thaxted and this 'over development' may also have been partly due to the rule of 'one Mass-day per altar'.

The font is 13th century having a 15th century oak cover. The altar chest placed on the east wall of the south transept is also 13th century and it has the earliest known paintings of oil on wood in the country. The church literature describes the chest as 'probably formerly the portable altar of a nobleman', which must speak volumes for the abilities of the carters of that era.

The Leper Stone

This large boulder was carried south by glaciers during the Anglian Ice Age (500,000 years ago), and it was deposited in its present position when the ice melted. Such boulders are referred to as 'erratics' and in this case it has become known as the 'Leper Stone'. It may be seen just north of St. Leonard's Close, on the eastern side of the B1383, grid reference TL 520 350.

The name 'Leper Stone' may have originated (somewhat erroneously), from the construction in 1207 of a hospice which was built immediately adjacent to it, on the present site of the horticultural Nursery, by Richard Serlo; 'for the benefit of the souls of his parents' (named as Serlo and Scholastica). The Hospice was dedicated to St. Mary and St. Leonard, the latter being the patron saint of lepers. However the hospice was never used as a leper hospital. It was later demolished and some of the stones from the original building have since been used to construct the wall forming the boundary of the nursery [2].

St Helen's Chapel

This Chapel was at one time known as St. Elene's Chapel and it is sited in what was once the manor of Bonhunt (or Bonant). It is believed to be Saxon and to have been built in the 11th century [1]. There is some evidence of work being done on two of the windows in the Norman style [5]. The Chapel was a private one and in 1340 it was known to be used by John Flambard of the manor of Bonhunt and his dependants. However after the Dissolution of the Monasteries it is thought that the building became derelict until about 1905, when it was used as a cattle shed and hen house. Presently it appears to be closed up.

Excavations in 1970 and 1993 unearthed a large cemetery extending both outside and inside the Chapel. The earlier find comprised 240 skeletons aligned east to west (signifying Christian burials), which it is thought could be dated from the middle Saxon period [1]. They were mostly male and 21 of the 240 skeletons showed severe battle injuries and 4 had been beheaded. The dig in 1993 (adjacent to the motorway), unearthed a further 51 skeletons, which also had Christian burials.

Many digs have been carried out in the area around the Chapel, grid reference TL 5113 3349. There is evidence of a flint industry which was operating in the Mesolithic period (around 11 000 BC) and those who reported on their finds have suggested that the valley floor may then have contained a lake. Finds from the Neolithic period (3000-1800 BC approx.) include pottery and hearths and evidence of a mixed economy of crop farming and hunting and indications of temporary accommodation. Carbon dating carried out on pottery unearthed in the dig of 1967 showed that it was manufactured in AD 830 (±50 years) and on this occasion 28 structures, including huts, barns, drains and two wells were found [6]. The pottery came from Peterborough, Ipswich and the Continent. Evidence was found of a break in occupation from around the ninth to the 11th centuries and this may have been directly due to the Viking raids which took place in 870 AD. Essex was regained in 918 AD, when the Danes inhabiting Cambridge surrendered to Edward the Elder.

The Church of All Saints Rickling

The earliest surviving part of the church is centered around a 13th century lancet window, which can only be seen from inside as it is situated in what is now the internal wall of the tower, which was added around 1340. However it is thought that the size of the nave suggests a pre-Conquest plan and visitors may be intrigued by the fact that the chancel which was also built around 1340 is assymmetrical to the nave. In the chancel is an oak chest with encompassing iron bands and a sturdy hasp, which was probably used to store details of births marriages and deaths. It was once covered in leather and dates from the 17th century. In the vestry is an engraved slate which is dedicated to the memory of Robert Turner who died in 1657. The reason for his death might concievably be inferred from the good practical advice which forms part of the inscription on the slate:

> *"It was the Deceased's advice to the Lyveinge that Noe man should suffer 110 ounces of blood to be taken from him".*

For the record, the visitor's book contains many entries which refer to the atmosphere of peace and quiet to be experienced within the church.

Details of Walk 5

Walk 5 covers an area mainly to the west of Newport and walk 6 covers an area mainly to the east; both walks take in short sections of the Harcamlow Way, which delineates approximately 225 km (140 miles) of footpaths, following the 'low' route from Harlow to Cambridge.

Map required:
Ordnance Survey Pathfinder Map No. 1050 (TL 43/53)
Saffron Walden 1:25 000.
Starting and finishing point:
Newport Station
Grid reference TL 523 336.

The prescribed walk following the red arrows.
Distance covered
9.7 km (6 miles)
Duration of walk
3 h 30 min. including a 30 min. break.

Saint Helen's Chapel - Wicken Bonhunt

Monk's Barn - Newport

Condition of terrain:
Generally firm and somewhat stony. Some outgoing sections of London Lane can be muddy.

The prescribed walk following the red and green arrows (viewing the Leper stone)
Distance covered
11.3 km (7 miles).
Duration of walk
4 h. including a 30 min. break.
Condition of terrain:
Generally firm and somewhat stony. Some outgoing sections of London Lane can be muddy.

The prescribed walk as above but also visiting Rickling Green.
Distance covered
12.9 km (8 miles).
Duration of walk
4 h 30 min. including a 30 min. break.
Condition of terrain:
Generally firm and somewhat stony. Some outgoing sections of London Lane can be muddy.

The shorter walk following the green arrows
Distance covered
3.5 km (2.2 miles)
Duration of walk
1 h 45 min. including a 30 min. break
Condition of terrain:
Generally firm and relatively smooth.

Places of Refreshment:
Newport has several public houses, two situated in the northern part of the town are `The White Horse' and `The Coach and Horses' which dates from the second half of the 16th century. The `Cricketer's Arms' is at Rickling Green.

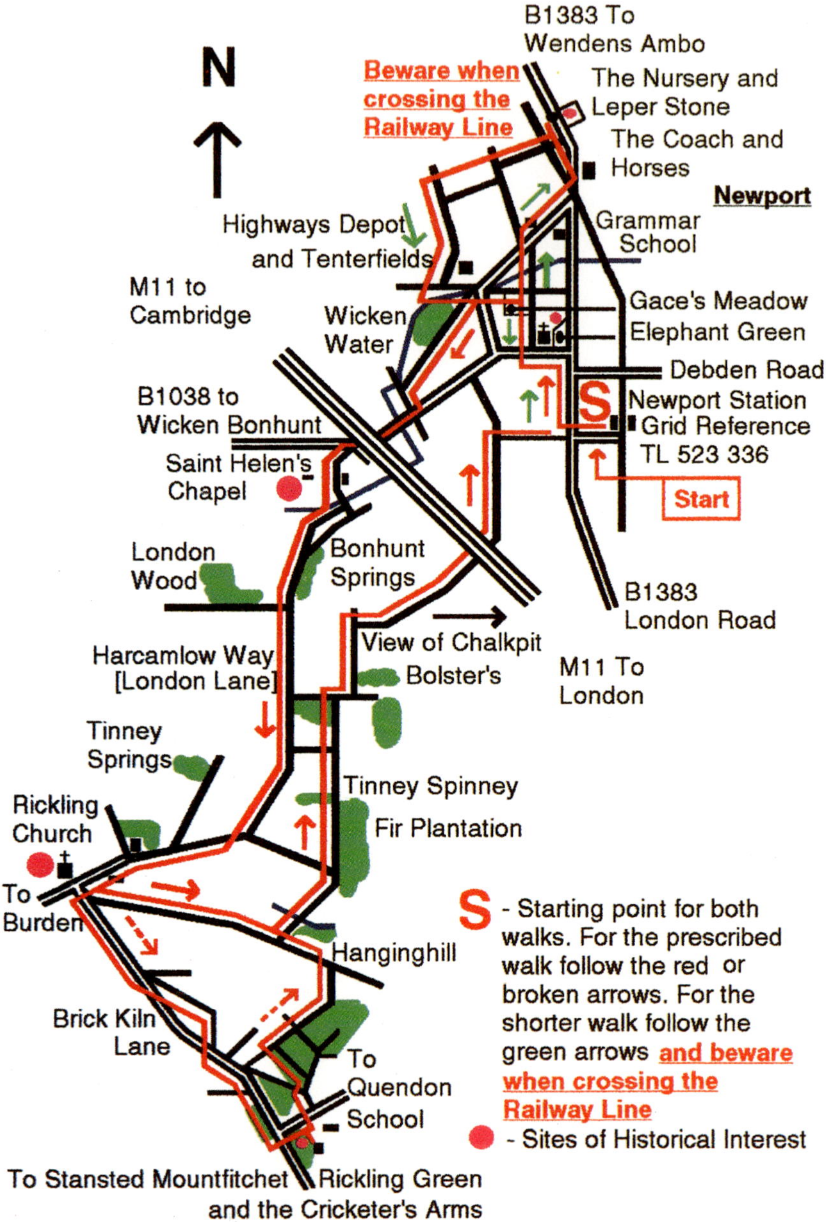
N
B1383 To
Wendens Ambo
Beware when
crossing the
Railway Line
The Nursery and
Leper Stone
The Coach and
Horses
Newport
Highways Depot
and Tenterfields
Grammar
School
M11 to
Cambridge
Wicken
Water
Gace's Meadow
Elephant Green
Debden Road
B1038 to
Wicken Bonhunt
S
Newport Station
Grid Reference
TL 523 336
Start
Saint Helen's
Chapel
London
Wood
Bonhunt
Springs
B1383
London Road
View of Chalkpit
Harcamlow Way
[London Lane]
Bolster's
M11 To
London
Tinney
Springs
Tinney Spinney
Rickling
Church
Fir Plantation
To
Burden
S - Starting point for both walks. For the prescribed walk follow the red or broken arrows. For the shorter walk follow the green arrows and beware when crossing the Railway Line
Hanginghill
Brick Kiln
Lane
To
Quendon
School
- Sites of Historical Interest
To Stansted Mountfitchet
Rickling Green
and the Cricketer's Arms

Walk 5

A long distance prehistoric trackway from the river Thames to the Fenland basin followed the valleys of the rivers Stort and the Cam via Stansted, Rickling, Bonhunt Water, Newport, Wendens Ambo and Chesterford [1]. Parts of this walk follow this ancient route which on the sketch map is also delineated as the Harcamlow Way.

The following quote [2], is useful in defining the direction of the 'old' route from Newport to London before the A11 (now the B1383), was constructed. My comments are contained within the square brackets.

> "Until the eighteenth century this road [the old road to London] came over the fields from Rickling church (now London Lane), turned east along the Wicken Road to avoid marshland, and continued round by the Church, through Elephant Green, alongside the modern A11 [now the B1383] (where the Western footpath marks the old level),....."

All Walkers

If walkers intend to visit the Church in Newport, obviously they should do so when their boots are free from mud and in order to facilitate this, it is recommended that the walk should be started from the station following the arrows on the sketch map, along Station Road and turning right into the High Street.

On the eastern side of the High Street is Pond Cross farm and until the late 18th century the remains of the old market cross were to be found beside the road, indicating that a market was held nearby [2]. According to D I Gordon the site of the market would have been adjacent to Newport 'pond', which covered the present Common and surroundings, but which dried up in the 16th century. However according to Bernard Nurse and Joy Pugh [1], markets were held in the Northern part of the village and at Elephant Green. It is possible that markets were held at different times at all three locations, perhaps with the oldest site being adjacent to the old market cross.

The timber framed and plastered property on the east side of the High Street (just before Debden Road), was used as a vicarage from the early 16th century until the middle of the 19th century and the last incumbent was the Reverend John Chapman, who (some say), haunts it still.

Also on the eastern side of the High Street (just north of Debden Road), is 'Monk's Barn', parts of which were believed to have been built in the late 15th or early 16th centuries when it was used by the monks of Saint Martin's le Grand in London (who had jurisdiction over the Church of Saint Mary), for use as a priest's 'house of retreat' [2]. An old carving of the Virgin and Child (with accompanying angels), may be seen positioned underneath an upper window.

To approach the Church, walkers should turn left into Wicken Street and then right into Church Street. According to information obtained by Joy Pugh from a transcription of a map of 1786 [1], the town cage (or lock-up) for offenders against the law was sited at the junction of Church Street and Elephant Green.

Taking the footpath on the western side of the church and proceeding in a northerly direction, leads to Gace's meadow on the left. Around 1529, upon the death of the owners of Gace's Farm (John and Agnes Covyle), Gace's Charity was set up to be administered by Trustees. The benefits of the Charity were to go mainly to the Church to provide requiem masses for the souls of the originators, with any remaining money being used for the payment of the King's Tax (or lay subsidy), on behalf of all the inhabitants of Newport. Most bequests to the Church of this nature were seized by Henry VIII at the time of the Reformation, but because the Charity was administered by Trustees it was allowed to continue and is still in operation today, while the King's tax was discontinued in the 17th century.

At Gace's Meadow the walkers can divide. Those who wish to view the Leper Stone should cross the bridge over Bury water and follow the green arrow on the sketch map turning right into Bury Water Lane (passing the grammar school), then left into the Cambridge Road. The stone is situated approximately 500 m (550 yds) north of the junction, on the right hand side of the road just past the 'Coach and Horses'.

In order to rejoin the main route walkers should cross the road from the Leper Stone, going back the way they came, when they will see a signposted footpath pointing Westwards along the boundary fence of a bungalow whose back garden contains an intriguing collection of bric a brac. **Take especial care when crossing the railway line!** The footpath continues across and down the side of the grammar school playing fields and back to Bury Water Lane, rejoining the prescribed route at 'Tenterfields'.

For those walkers who do not wish to view the Leper Stone and intend to follow **the prescribed walk following the red arrows,** they should not cross the bridge but should turn left (east), at the end of Gace's meadow and then follow the course of Wicken Water (known locally as Bury Water), in a westerly direction as far as the bridge at the junction of School Lane and Bury Water Lane (opposite to the Council Highways Depot).

According to Joy Pugh [1], cloth woven in the town was fulled (cleaned of grease), by treading it in the water near the bridge, which at that time was a ford. After this process it was then stretched and held by 'tenterhooks' on frames set up in the 'tenterfield' after which the present housing estate has been named. The route then follows a footpath in a south westerly direction across the fields to join up with the B1038 (the Wicken Road). This road passes under the motorway and reference to the sketch map will show that Saint Helen's Chapel may then be approached by turning southwards.

The walk continues along the ancient trackway which is also part of the Harcamlow Way, to Rickling, named after Ricola, a late sixth century queen of Essex. At the time of the Black Death All Saints Church at Rickling was at the centre of the village, but it is now somewhat isolated as a result of the rapid migration at that time of the remaining healthy villagers to Rickling Green, which is approximately

2.4 km (1.5 miles) away by road and 2 km (1.25 miles) by footpath. Those wishing to visit Rickling Green and possibly the Cricketer's Arms, should now follow the dotted red arrows (shown on the sketch map), while those proposing to follow the (slightly shorter) prescribed route, should take the footpath going Eastwards from Brick Kiln Lane, following the red arrows to Hanginghill.

Rickling Green is the site of a cricket ground where W. G. Grace played and it is also the place where in 1882 a now defunct London social club 'The New Orlean's' scored 920 runs in one day against a local side. The visitor's team included some well chosen players, three of whom were ex County cricket captains and it was shortly after this match that the current rule of 'declaring' was invoked For cricketing buffs, it is understood that the owners of the Cricketer's Arms are planning to display a copy of the score book of the match on the Internet.

The return leg of the walk from Rickling Green is commenced by following the dotted red arrow towards Hanginghill. According to Jacqueline Cooper [7], some people who lived in Medieval times considered it to be something of a social cachet, if a gallows was erected on their land; clearly such an aspiration must have carried a hidden agenda, for those property owners who were less than completely law abiding.

The remainder of the walk takes place along footpaths which run roughly parallel to the ancient track, but which are situated a short distance to the east of it and it is quite probable that this route formed a handy alternative to the main track, at those times when the traffic was known to be heavier than usual, or the weather was bad, or in case of outbreaks of lawlessness. It should be noted that Wicken Road (part of the main track), was at one time considered to be 'a verrye naughtye waye' [2].

The latter part of the walk passes over some very stoney tracks and just past 'Bolsters' to the east there is a good view of the Chalkpit, showing evidence of the deposits of clay in surface crevasses due to the melting of ice at the time of the Anglian Ice Age.

References

1 Bernard Nurse, Joy Pugh, Imogen Mollet. A Village in Time, the history of Newport Essex, Publisher: Newport News (1995).

2 Gordon D.I. Dr. A brief history of the Village of Newport and it`s Church (1969) pps 6, 7, 8 and 12. Essex Record Office, box N1.

3 Eddy M.R. and Petchey M.R. Historic Towns in Essex. Essex County Council 1983.

4 Hayes J.W. A History of Newport. Essex Record Office Box N1.

5 Laver Henry, The Chapel of St. Elene at Wicken Bonhunt. Transactions of the Essex Archaeological Society IX New Series 1906 pages 404-407.

6 The Archaeology Section, Essex County Council Planning Department, County Hall, Chelmsford. Archaeology Assistant Ms Alison Bennett.

7 Cooper, Jacqueline and Peter, Discover Walden. Cooper Publications, 24 Pelham Road, Clavering, Saffron Walden.

Newport

Walk 6 - East of Newport

The Church of St. Mary and All Saints Debden

THE north and south sides of the church were built of rubble and flint between the dates of 1220 and 1245 and the brick construction was carried out during the 18th century. When the font was first made it was exhibited to King George III at Buckingham Palace and was also described and illustrated in The European Magazine in the year 1786. The enormous iron strapped chest dates from the 14th century and is made of oak 75 mm (three inches) thick.

Mr. R.M.T. Chiswell helped finance many of the renovations which were carried out in the period between 1786-1792. His remains are buried in the vault and his tomb chest is contained in his chapel above it. Unfortunately he lost a great deal of money on speculative ventures in the West Indies and in 1797, he committed suicide [1].

Details of Walk 6

Map required:
Ordnance Survey Pathfinder Map No. 1050 (TL 43/53) Saffron Walden 1:25 000.

Starting and finishing point:
Newport Station
Grid reference TL 523 336.

The prescribed walk following the red arrows
Distance covered:
7.6 km (4.75 miles).
Duration of walk:
2 h 45 min. including a 30 minute break.
Condition of terrain:
Generally firm and relatively smooth.

The shorter walk following the green arrows.
Distance covered:
3 km (1.9 miles)
Duration of walk:
1 h 30 min. including a 30 min. break.
Condition of terrain:
Generally firm and relatively smooth.

Places of Refreshment:
Debden has two public houses the White Hart and the Plough

Shaped flints (currently held in Saffron Walden Museum) providing evidence of the existence of hunters from the Mesolithic Period (around 11000 BC), were found on a terrace of chalk 400 m (0.25 miles), south east of Newport station at grid reference TL 525 330. Later, arrowheads, many other flint tools and pottery, dating from the Neolithic Period (3000-1800 BC approx.) and from the Bronze Age (2000-1000 BC approx.), were recovered from a field south

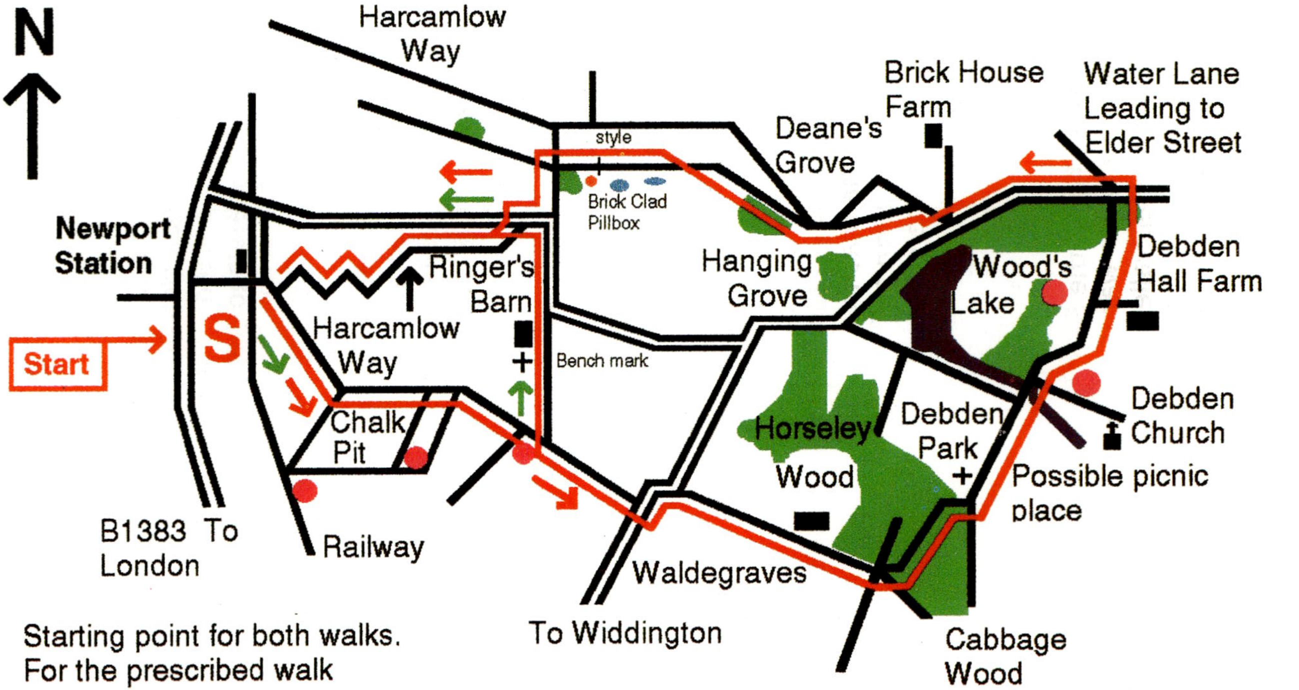

S Starting point for both walks. For the prescribed walk follow the red arrows. For the shorter walk follow the green arrows

● Sites of Historical interest.

Walk 6

of the chalk pit on a steep bluff above the level ground that was once Newport pond at grid reference TL 5275 3307[2]. This same area was also once the site of a windmill which is marked on Chapman and Andre's map of 1897.

The area where Newport is now sited was covered by sea water on two occasions and during these periods layers of chalk were deposited. This occurred between about 445 and 415 million years ago (the Silurian Period) and from 100 to 2 million years ago (the Cretaceous and Tertiary periods). Subsequently, with the coming of the Anglian Ice Age (500,000 years ago), glaciers covered the area and when these melted, layers of clay were then deposited on top of the chalk, filling in any cracks which were present. The resulting wedge like formations can be seen on the vertical sides of the chalk quarry.

The site of Widdington windmill is marked on Chapman and Andre's map of 1897 and it's position is shown on the sketch map just before the tee junction connecting with Ringer's Barn grid reference TL 5320 3317. All that remains of the site is a circular swelling of the ground; this can be seen when the earth is bare, but it may not be visible when crops are growing.

Those walkers who have elected to follow the shorter walk should now turn in a northerly direction towards the bench mark and Ringer's Barn and continue following the green arrows as shown on the sketch map.

Just off the road from Widdington to Debden lies Waldegrave's farm and farmhouse, the latter being currently boarded up. The farm is named after a Sir William Waldegrave who was given Mole Hall (grid reference TL 549 314), by Henry VIII in 1510.

The walk continues into the Parish of Debden or 'Deppedana' as it was recorded by the Normans in the Domesday book; the Saxon name for the town was Dependuna which was derived from two Saxon words meaning a 'deep valley'.

The Parish was once owned by a Saxon called Seward, who after the Norman conquest was dispossessed of his property and lands, which were then given to Ralph Peverill, after whom Peverel's Wood was named, (grid reference TL 555 354). In 1153 a grandson of Ralph poisoned the Earl of Chester and after fleeing the country he in his turn was dispossessed by King Henry II who in 1214, gave the manor of Debden Hall to his son, who later became King John.

For those walkers who might like to visit Debden Church and possibly the White Hart (and/or the Plough), a short detour is required, in the course of which another 'erratic' (a stone deposited when glaciers melted), may be seen to the north side of the footpath. It is approximately 0.8 m high X 0.8 m wide X 1.0 m long, (grid reference TL 5505 3325).

Returning to the scheduled route, Debden Hall farm is approached, to the west of which was the site of Debden Hall built in the 14th century and demolished in 1936 [1].

After passing Debden Hall Farm the footpath (which is the original driveway to and from Debden Hall) joins Water Lane, this being a probable extension of the Roman road referred to as 'Elder Street' running eastwards towards Radwinter. This same Roman Road also ran westwards towards the place now known as Newport [3], but it is not clear whether the route followed the existing Debden Road, or whether it followed Bromley Lane on the northern slope of the Debden Water valley, joining into what is now known as Harcamlow Way (by the sewage works); or whether it followed the line of the footpath on the southern side of the valley, passing through Chalkpit Plantation.

After moving westwards along Water Lane, walkers should leave the road at the entrance to Brick House Farm and follow the line of Debden Water for approximately 1000 m (0.6 mile), when on the south side of their track they will notice some irregularly shaped mounds of earth remaining from disused pit workings. After crossing a style, passing a brick clad concrete pillbox and passing under some power lines (a distance of approximately 300 m (330 yds) past these mounds), they should then turn south, taking the footpath which is part of the Harcamlow Way and which leads rather steeply up the side of the valley and across the Debden Road back to the starting point of the walk.

References

1 Norwak J.M. The Parish of Debden and the Church of St. Mary and All Saints. Essex Record Office box D2.

2 The Archaeology Section, Essex County Council Planning Department, County Hall, Chelmsford. Archaeology Assistant Ms Alison Bennett.

3 Bassett S.R. Saffron Walden: excavation and research 1972-80 (1982), page 8 and figure 2.

Little Dunmow and Stebbing

Walk 7

Little Dunmow

LITTLE Dunmow and Stebbing are each mentioned in the Domesday Book. Both Little Dunmow and Great Dunmow are referred to as 'Dommauua' and Stebbing as 'Stibinga'. During the reign of Edward the Confessor (1042-1066), Little Dunmow was held by a woman called Ailish. In her time she was referred to as a 'freewoman', a term which implied that she was in a privileged position enjoying both political and civil liberties. After the Norman Conquest the Manor was awarded to a follower of William the Conqueror a Ralph Baynard, who at that time already held 25 Lordships in Essex alone. His grandson William was involved later in an attempted rebellion against King Henry I and his estates were then confiscated. The manor of Little Dunmow was handed to Richard Fitzgilbert, the founder of the Fitzwalter family and this dynasty held the manor for 10 generations, extending over a period of 300 years [1]. Effigies of the last Fitzwalter male and his wife (who died in 1464), may be seen in the usual recumbent position on top of the double tomb in the Priory Church.

One member of the family, Robert Fitzwalter, was the leader of the barons who in 1215 were jointly responsible for the production and signing of the Magna Carta, this defined the baron's feudal obligations to the monarchy, confirmed the liberties of the English Church and for the first time limited the power of the King. The Charter later evolved into a statement of Civil Rights.

Some of those who were associated with the manor of Little Dunmow had their share of misfortune and one of these was Thomas Radcliffe who was killed in the wars of the Roses. In 1485 his son was given a peerage by Henry VII and he became Baron Fitzwalter; but was later beheaded for his part in a Yorkist plot, which was referred to as the 'Perkin Warbeck conspiracy'. In 1620 another owner of the manor Sir Henry Mildmay, was appointed by James I of England to be the Master of the King's Jewel House. However during the two Civil Wars fought in the reign of Charles I, Sir Henry was not on the side of the monarchy. In fact he was present at the King's trial 1n 1649 and later during the Commonwealth he served as a State Councillor. When in 1660 the system of monarchy was restored, Mildmay was ordered to account for the Crown jewels which he presumably found difficult, for he tried to escape, was captured and sentenced to life imprisonment and while on his way to being transported to Tangier, he died in Antwerp.

The Priory Church of St. Mary the Virgin Little Dunmow.

Visitors to the church will find the items of historical interest all clearly labelled and described. The present church is the remaining part of a much larger building which served as a place of worship for a group of Augustinian monks. They lived in a Priory which was founded in 1104 by Lady Juga, a sister of Ralph Baynard. At the time of the foundation, the Priory was endowed with half a hide of land. The 'hide' was an Anglo Saxon measurement of area and it was used in the calculation of tax assessments. In true 'Alice in Wonderland' style its size varied from place to place. For instance on Royal Manors it represented a much larger area than it did on other properties, thus lowering the amount of tax required on Royal lands and conversely increasing it for the others [2]. The area could vary from 16 to 49 hectare (40 to 120 acres), so making it a very flexible and convenient measurement for the exchequer. It is tempting to suggest that the area represented by half a hide at the Priory may just have been rather small, as in 1369 a writ was served on one of the canons, a William De Stoke, for counterfeiting the King's money!

Robert Fitzwalter (of Magna Carta fame), had a daughter Matilda, who is reputed to be the 'Maid Marion' who subsequently married Robin Hood; later taking his title and becoming the Countess of Huntingdon. She was at one time believed to be buried in the tomb surmounted by the effigy of a young woman in the Priory Church. However it is now considered that the date of the tomb is much later [1]. A considerable legend has grown up about Matilda and for those who enjoy a good story written in a style which would not disgrace the brothers Grimm, the relevant text may be found in 'Notes, Antiquarian, Topographical No. 1' by J.F.R. in the Graphic Illustrator [3].

The Priory at Little Dunmow is famed for the holding of the Flitch Trials. According to the Dunmow Official Guide [4], these were known at the time of Henry III (1216-1272) and involved the award of a flitch of bacon to any man (women were not allowed in the Priory), who 'repented not of his marriage, sleeping or waking, in a year and a day' and who also took an oath while kneeling on two rough corbel stones. These can be seen inside the church near the altar.

The Oath

"You shall swear by Custom of Confession
That you ne'er made Nuptial Transgression
Nor since you were married Man and Wife,
By Household Brawls or Contentious Strife,
Or otherwise in Bed or att board
Offended each other in deed or word;
Or in a twelve month time and a day,
Repented not in Thought any way;
Or since the Church clerk said Amen
Wish'd yourselves unmarried again
But continued true, and in desire
As when you joined hand in holy Choir."

It is presumed that this ritual was instituted in order to encourage local members of the lay public to join the marital state, rather than just to take a common law spouse.

The aspirations outlined above had not gone unnoticed by Chaucer in the 14th century, when he wrote the following words in the Canterbury Tales:

"The Bacon was not fet for hem, I trow,
That Som men have in Essex at Dunmow"

The Dunmow Official Guide also quotes from Howell, a 16th century writer as follows:

"Do not Fetch your wife from Dunmow
For so you may bring home two sides of a sow."

The only safe way to comment on such a sentiment is to echo the words of the character Frances Urquhart in the television plays 'To Play The King' and 'The Final Cut' by Michael Dobbs; when he says:

"You might well say that, but I could not possibly comment."

The Priory church contains the oak chair in which the successful claimants of the 'flitch' were subsequently chaired through the streets. The Flitch ceremony has not been re-enacted every year since its inception, but it has been 'revived' from time to time. The ceremony currently takes place in Dunmow Town Hall having been 'hijacked' from Little Dunmow on July 19th 1855. There is a long and detailed account of the proceedings and the events leading up to them in the Illustrated London News dated 28th July 1855 [5].

The Dunmow Flitch Chair kept at The Priory Church of Saint Mary the Virgin - Little Dunmow

Stebbing

Stebbing lies on the northern side of Stane Street, the Roman road linking Dunmow with Colchester and along which Roman remains have been found. In the fifth century the Saxon clan of Stybba are reputed to have settled in the 'ing' or meadow of 'Stibinga' and approximately five centuries after that, during the reign of Edward the Confessor (1042-1066), the Normans relieved Siward the Saxon owner, of his property in Stibinga, dividing the area into two. Stebbing Park was given to Henry de Ferrers (one of whose relations was engaged in the compilation of the Domesday Book) and the rest to Ralph Peverell, (whose son later founded the priory at Hatfield Peverel).

The Black Death reached southern England in 1348 and was prevalent for about two years, before moving Northwards. The disease killed off so many people that labour became short and for the first time workers on the land discovered that they could command payment for their services. The Landowners quickly found that one way of making arable farming less labour intensive, was to keep sheep and hence during those times, the villages in the southern part of the country gradually became producers of wool and cloth; although there is no evidence of weaving for commercial purposes taking place in Stebbing [6].

From the 16th century to the middle of the 19th century the administration of public services was carried out by members of the 'Vestry'; a group of people charged with keeping the peace, keeping the roads repaired and keeping the poor. The nearest 'House of Correction' was at Newport, so that a temporary place of confinement was needed for law breakers which was referred to as the 'Cage'. Vestry records at Stebbing show that the proceeds from the sale of two cottages (left to them for the benefit of the poor), were used to help finance the construction of such a cage; which may not have been quite what was intended by those who bequeathed the cottages! Much time was spent in returning poor people to their parish of origin, so that the expense of looking after them did not fall on local resources and some paupers were even given help towards the cost of emigrating to Australia.

An interesting extract from the Session Rolls of Chelmsford dated 1645 is as follows:

"Richard Pettit, baker, of Little Dunmow,laid information against 11 people for trading as bakers without being apprenticed thereunto - whereby each has forfeited 40 shillings, of which sum the informer sues for half."

Even more interestingly in the same year, the same Richard Pettit is again recorded as informing on a further 16 people for the same offence!

No description of the life and times of Stebbing would be complete without some reference being given to the experiences and recollections of Frank Howland, who for many years owned and operated Church Farm. His description of some of the brewing methods used before the cost of a licence to brew went up from nine shillings per year to 16 pounds per year, is taken from reference[7] and repeated here by kind permission of his son David Howland.

"When we brewed at Church End, we always got the water from the horse pond, where the horses used to walk in up to their bellies to drink. The cattle also did the same, as we had no water mains in those days. I expect the water from the springs was too hard for brewing, but I could never bring myself to drink the stuff, especially when you had some horses with greasy heels.
Of course it was well boiled, and the men loved it. We used to get 54 gallon casks from the brewery which had had bulk brandy in them, and I expect some of the brandy was left in (the retail price of whiskey was only 24 shillings a gallon then) - and this was the way we stored our beer."

Could the change in the licence fee have been the start of

the proliferation of public houses? Mr Howland goes on to recall that a neighbouring farmer who also used his horsepond as a water supply for brewing, used to throw two sheep's heads into the pond, 14 days before he extracted the water; this was said to prevent the beer from being cloudy! Another quote from the same source gives a description of the way in which the beer was consumed:

> *"We always brewed before harvest and allowed one gallon of home brewed beer a day for each man, and they never had enough. They would start work in the harvest-time at five o'clock in the morning, begin with a quart of beer for each man, and then have breakfast at eight o'clock. Most of them would not drink tea as they said it caused internal rust but they were always ready to drink another quart of beer when coming back to work.*
> *At eleven o'clock they would have 'Elevenses' with more beer in a twenty-minute break, then at one o'clock there would be dinner and more beer. They went back to work at two o'clock and at four o'clock there would be a tea break, which I used to call a beer break. Most of their gallon bottles would be empty by then and they would ask for more beer, which we were allowed to give them. By the end of the day they were as full of this strong old beer as it was possible to carry, and a more disagreeable lot you never saw, and by the next morning they were like bears with sore heads."*

Half way between Stebbing and Great Saling is Andrew's Field, which was used by the Americans during the Second World War as an airfield from which Flying Fortresses and Marauders operated. Stebbing Church was on the flight path and Mr Howland recollects that 'they took off with their loads of bombs over Stebbing with a terrible noise, sometimes just missing the church.'

The Church of St. Mary the Virgin Stebbing.

This church like the Priory church at Little Dunmow and the church at 'Church End' Great Dunmow, is also dedicated to St. Mary The Virgin, so some care is needed to avoid possible confusion! The present church was built about 1324, though a church had been present in Stebbing before 1086 as it is recorded in the Domesday Book that "there has always been there one priest" [8].

The period from 1552-1559 was a time of religious upheaval, referred to as 'The Reformation' and it touched on the reigns of three Monarchs, Edward VI (1547-1553), Mary I (1553-1558) and Elizabeth I (1558-1603). Edward was a Protestant and he changed the religion practised in the Church from Roman Catholic to Protestant. Mary was a Catholic and she reversed the process, while Elizabeth who was a Protestant, again reverted to Protestantism! It is understandable that churchwardens all over the country would at that time have developed considerable inertia to any further changes; with the result that in 1643 the Earl of Manchester, who was General of the Eastern Counties, obtained a warrant to enable a William Dowsing to carry out acts of demolition of brass inscriptions, Popish idols, crosses and any cherubims that could be found, in or around the churches in Cambridge and Suffolk. In fact it is thought that his attentions were also turned towards some Essex churches, where it is stated that some people refused to raise ladders [8]. However at this time many of the coloured glass windows in the church at Stebbing were destroyed, being later replaced with plain glass.

The Church of Saint Mary the Virgin - Stebbing

Details of Walk 7

Map required:
Ordnance Survey Pathfinder No. 1075 (TL 62/72) Great Dunmow and Braintree 1: 25 000.
Starting and finishing point:
Little Dunmow Priory Church
Grid reference TL 656 212.

Distance covered:
11.27 km (7 miles).
Duration of walk:
4h 30 min. including a 1h break
Condition of terrain:
Generally firm.
That part of the walk marked A-B is generally rather rough with nettles in the months of June, July and the early part of August.

Places of Refreshment:
In Little Dunmow there is the Dunmow Flitch public house.
In Stebbing there is a choice of at least three public houses.

If walkers intend visiting either the Church at Little Dunmow, or the church at Stebbing, it is suggested that it would be socially responsible to avoid doing so with muddy boots!

Two Roman coins bearing the heads of Alectus and Tacitus were found in the garden of one of the cottages close to Little Dunmow Priory Church at grid reference TL 655 212. The fishponds (now dry), which once served the Priory, are on private property. They are marked on the sketch map and parts of them may be seen on the western side of the footpath leading in a southerly direction towards the dis-used railway line. The walk takes in a short section of the old line including Felsted Station, where digs have unearthed evidence of a Roman villa and other dwelling places dating

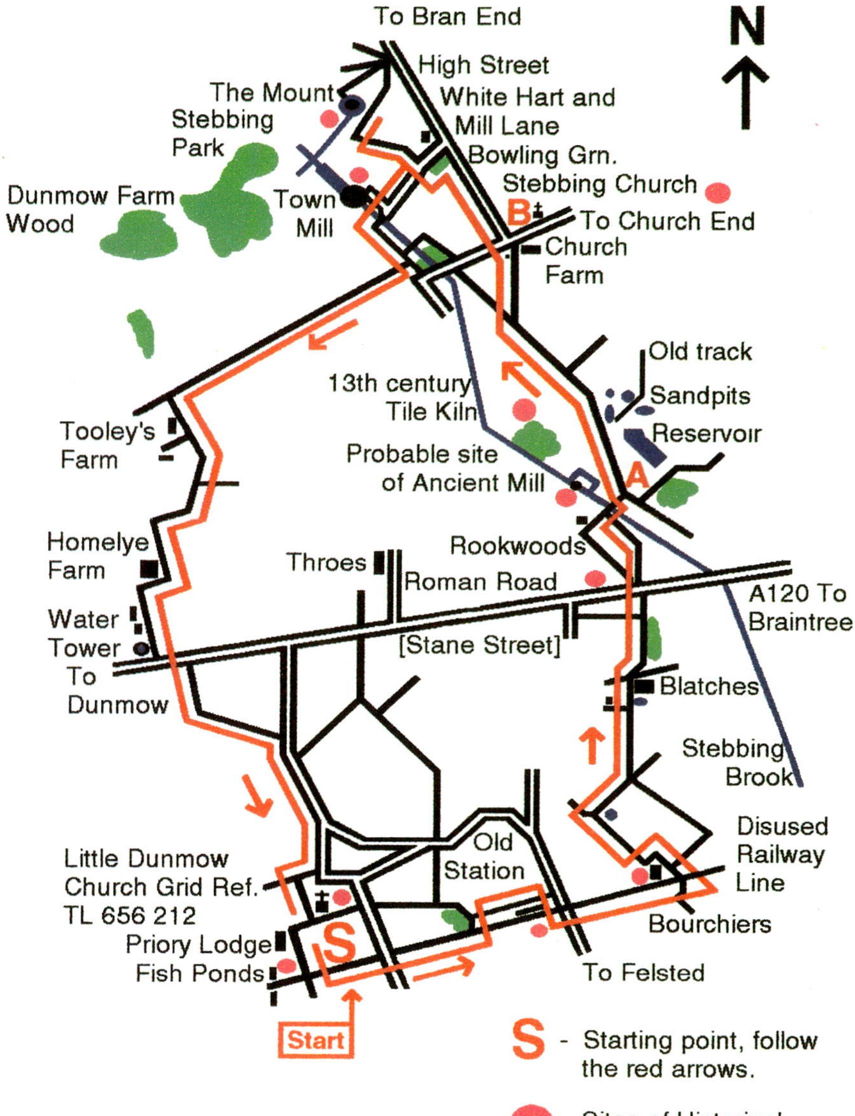
To Bran End
N
High Street
The Mount
White Hart and
Mill Lane
Stebbing
Park
Bowling Grn.
Dunmow Farm
Wood
Town
Mill
Stebbing Church
B
To Church End
Church
Farm
Old track
13th century
Tile Kiln
Sandpits
Tooley's
Farm
Reservoir
Probable site
of Ancient Mill
A
Homelye
Farm
Rookwoods
Throes
Roman Road
A120 To
Braintree
Water
Tower
[Stane Street]
To
Dunmow
Blatches
Stebbing
Brook
Disused
Railway
Line
Old
Station
Little Dunmow
Church Grid Ref.
TL 656 212
Bourchiers
Priory Lodge
S
Fish Ponds
To Felsted
Start
S - Starting point, follow the red arrows.
Sites of Historical Interest
A-B See text.

Walk 7

from the first four centuries AD, including 'native' and Roman pottery of the Claudian era and two Roman silver coins of Antoninus Pius and Constantine I.

When ecavations were made at Bourchiers, Roman pottery, 18 coins, a Roman iron axe and two small mid first century flasks of 'grey ware' were discovered, all of which may be seen in Colchester museum. The house at Blatches Farm was once the boyhood home of Lionel Lukin who later became a coach builder to the wealthier inhabitants of London. Is it a coincidence that 'Blatches' is itself well served by metalled tracks which would be eminently suited to the passage of horse drawn carriages? Lukin was a friend of the Prince Regent who encouraged him to develop his ideas for an 'unimmergible lifeboat' and it is reputed that the pond in Great Dunmow was used by him to test his ideas for a suitable craft. More information on Lionel Lukin is given in the text of walk 8.

The walk continues north of Blatches crossing the Roman Road Stane Street. Interestingly, investigations carried out over a short section of the road to the west of the crossing point have shown that the Roman road was laid on top of an ancient well ballasted track.

The footpath next crosses Stebbing Brook over a timber bridge followed by a stile and it is thought that near a point north west of Rookwoods was sited one of two old Stebbing watermills, called variously 'Kanonismelone', 'Canons Mill' and at other times 'Broom Mill' [9]. The first name is mentioned in a deed dated 1329 and it is suggested that the second name was changed to 'Broom Mill' at the time of the Dissolution of the Monasteries in order to avoid the attentions of Henry VIII and his commissioners! One of the fields nearby is still called 'the Brooms'. The mill was last mentioned in a record of a letting in 1634, but it was not shown on the map made by Chapman and Andre in 1775, neither is it mentioned in Peter Muilman's contemporaneous 'History of Essex'.

Traditionally Parish boundaries follow the course of rivers and this is mainly the case in this area. Reference to the

Pathfinder map will reveal that at grid reference TL 6635 2318 the boundary leaves the present course of Stebbing Brook and follows an absurdly convoluted path, subsequently rejoining the Brook further downstream. Mr. K. J. Ellis suggests that this may be taken as evidence of a deliberate re-routing of the Brook designed to make the operation of a water mill possible. The area around Rookwoods is also well served with footpaths and he goes on to point out that the track which passes between the sandpits and the reservoir also curves round in the direction of the supposed site of the mill, at which point it may have at one time terminated. Reference to the Ordnance Survey map will reveal that presently the track stops short of reaching the proposed site.

A 13th century tile kiln was situated to the west of the footpath and just north of the wood at grid reference TL 6645 2323.

Next the walk passes close by Church Farm which was once home to Frank Howland and is now farmed by his son David. Stebbing Church is to the east and walkers should pass along the High Street, turning left at the bowling green and into Mill Lane. Stebbing Mount which is privately owned, may be seen by taking the footpath leading in a north westerly direction from Mill Lane, but please do walk round the village cricket pitch, to exit through a wooden gate leading to a footpath over a stream. The Mount consists of a mound of earth having a flat top. It is approximately 9.5 m above the surrounding ground level and it is surrounded by a moat supplied with water from a spring. If it is visited in early March walkers will notice that its sides are covered in daffodils.

Tradition has it that a castle once occupied the site but the date is not specified [10]. Castles are expected to have an encircling moat in order to discourage invaders and in Essex there are many properties (other than castles), which are also surrounded by moats. It is not now thought that these moats were constructed specifically to deter human invaders, but were possibly of use in keeping wild animals from the surrounding forests away from the stacks, barns and dwelling places. Later on when most of the forests were converted to farmland, this danger would have been lessened and it is just possible that in some cases having a moat became a form of medieval 'keeping up with the Jones's'.

The walk now doubles back towards Mill Lane, at the end of which the Town Mill is sited. The front part of the present building is believed to be Victorian and it is thought that an earlier mill operated on the same site from the time of the Domesday Book in 1086. A reference in a deed dated 1316 refers to 'the road to the mill called Bullocksmele', the implication being that the road ended at the mill. Just such a road is the present day Mill Lane. Readers could also note that whenever a watermill is replaced it is extremely likely that the new building would have been erected on the same site, so making use of the existing waterways and sluice gates [9].

Output from the watermills seems to have been sufficient to deal with the local produce from the farms up to the early 18th century, for Chapman and Andre on their map of 1775 show the site of only one windmill, which was at Bran End. Over the years however other windmills were built and their sites have been carefully indicated and mapped by K J Ellis in reference[9].

The return part of the walk is via Tooley`s Farm and Homelye Farm past a Water Tower, ultimately returning to the Priory Church at Little Dunmow.

References

1 Jones Alan. A brief history of Little Dunmow. Essex Record Office box D3.

2 Powell W Raymond. Essex in Domesday Book. Essex Record Office 1990.

3 J.F.R. Notes, Antiquarian and Topographical No. 1-Priory Church, Little Dunmow, Essex, The Graphic Illustrator. Essex Record Office box D3.

4 Dunmow Official Guide. Essex Record Office box D3.

5 Extract from the Illustrated London News dated 28th July 1855. Essex Record Office box D3.

6 Holles Robert, Phillips, Mann and Kingdom, Stebbing The Prospect for Survival 1975. The Essex Record Office box S3.

7 Howland F. Stebbing, Memories of it's people their customs and habitats. 1972. Essex Record Office box S3.

8 Livesey C.E. Rev. The Church of St. Mary the Virgin Stebbing. 1924 The Essex Record Office Box S3.

9 Ellis K.J. A Guide to the Town Mill and a history of milling in Stebbing. The Essex Record Office Box S3.

10 Victoria County History. Volume I pp 302-304.

Great Dunmow

Walk 8

THE town of Great Dunmow has been known by many names. Dunemowe (Saxon about A.D.951), Dunnauue, or Dommawe, or Much Donnawe [1] and at the time of the Domesday survey it is recorded as Dommauua. Philip Morant writing in reference[2] mentions Dunemauee, Dunmaw, Dunmage, Dunmawge, Domauua, Dunmore, etc. He writes:

> *"the name of Dunmow feems naturally to be formed from the two Saxon words, Dun, a hill, and mop, an heap: implying, according to fome a raifed way: it ftanding upon the old caufey (causeway), or Roman road, that leads from Bifhop's Stortford to Colchefter."*

In 1086 the total number of households in Dunmow was 72 and in Chelmsford there were four, with Moulsham having 26. It is interesting to note that archaeologists have established that the Roman road Stane Street, is itself built on top of an ancient track which runs from west to east towards the coast.

In 1253 King Henry III issued a 'Charter' granting the right to John de Berners to hold a market in Much Donnawe on Saturdays. Predictably this took place in the town centre in Market Place, where the stocks and town pump were situated. The present pump which once had a horse-trough adjacent to it, is now sited in the High street. Later in 1555, during the reign of Philip and Mary the town was given the status of a Borough and this was confirmed in 'letters patent' by Queen Elizabeth I in 1590. The corporation of the borough comprised thirteen burgesses, from whose number one Bailiff was elected. The by-laws produced by these presumably worthy citizens were somewhat draconian, as shown in the following selection taken from 'Dunmow Through the Ages' by Dorothy C Dowsett.

> *"No man shall take in a lodger or let his house without first acquainting the corporation. Every person to pay a fine before being allowed to dwell in the town. If any person deryed, scorne, mocke, rayle at the Bailiff or burgesses he shall be fined 6/8d. No apprentice, servant or journeyman to be out after 9 o`clock. Everyone to pay the rates levied by the corporation or forfeit double. All unmarried persons not having an honest vocation to be brought before a justice."*

Unhappily, by an Act of Parliament decreed in 1885 Dunmow ceased to be a Borough, as at that time the population was less than 5000. However copies of both Charters may be seen on the north wall of the Church of Saint Mary The Virgin at Church End (or ye Churcheyend as it was known in 1549).

Shortly after 1570 when Flemish refugees first came to this country (settling initially in Colchester), the people of Dunmow set up a cottage industry making two kinds of cloth called 'bay' and 'say'. Bay was a coarse woollen cloth which could readily be made into blankets, the nap of which was raised by using locally grown teasels. Say was a much finer serge like material, which could be made into shirts and linings. The road referred to as 'Tenterfields' on the sketch map runs adjacent to the fields where the produce was first washed in the waters of the river Chelmer and then hung on 'tenterhooks'. Such an activity is also known to have occurred in the area of Newport (see walk 6). The advent of mechanical weaving in the northern part of the country resulted in a decline in home produced cloth in the south and by the end of the 18th century the industry had become moribund, causing much hardship.

Apart from agricultural pursuits the people of Dunmow also took part in the tanning of leather and this is known to have taken place in at least four places around the town and these have been identified in [1]. Subsequently the tanning trade also declined due to the establishment of the processes on a factory basis in other areas in this country and abroad.

Readers may care to note that in 1535 Thomas Cromwell (Chancellor of the Exchequer to Henry VIII), required all details of baptisms, marriages and deaths of the local populace to be entered into a Register, which was to be kept in a secure place in every church. This requirement was viewed with a great deal of cynicism simply because it was perceived that such details might then be used to raise the level of taxation; (clearly the aims of government do not change). In Dunmow the request was tacitly ignored and three years later, Cromwell issued a decree making it mandatory for such records to be kept by every vicar and curate in the land. From this time in Dunmow a record of Baptisms was kept, but a register of Marriages and Burials did not start until 1558 [6]. The resulting Parish Registers have since proved to be a very useful and reliable data bank for genealogists and historians.

For the record in 1509 the Manor of Great Dunmow and Dunmow Park formed part of Katherine of Aragon's 'dower' (dowry) when she married King Henry VIII.

Most communities suffered from death dealing plagues and Dunmow was no exception. Dorothy Dowsett uses information from the Parish Registers to show that in 1609 five people died of 'the peste', which may or may not have been due to the Bubonic plague. This plague certainly struck on three separate occasions. In 1603 48 persons died, in 1625 23 persons died and in 1665 38 persons died. I find it interesting to note that in 1620 a building up for sale in Dunmow was described as being in 'Dedmans Lane' and it seems likely that this lane was associated with deaths from the plague (and later from smallpox), as it was not until about 100 years ago that the name of the thoroughfare was changed to its present name 'Saint Edmunds Lane'. A map of the town for the year 1894, shows the road as 'Deadman's Lane' and also shows the position of the Pest House, where it is also possible that communal burials of the victims of the various plagues may have taken place.

Most local charities were centred around the church and the Gilds (Guilds). The Gilds were the medieval equivalent of mutual benefit societies, the function of which was to cushion their members from the possible effects of economic deprivation, sickness and old age. Their connections with the church also ensured that masses could be said for individuals whenever it was considered to be necessary. Due to bequests and legacies the Gilds became wealthy and rich in property and in 1545, by order of Henry VIII all these assets were appropriated. This despicable act destroyed the ability of the members of the Gild to help those of their colleagues who had fallen on hard times and it is from this moment that alms boxes began to appear in churches.

In spite of this and many other hostile acts against both the Church and the Gilds the local churchwarden`s account book [1], contains the following entry:

> *"1561 payd to the good wife Barker for ale for them that dyd rynge when the Queene's grace cam thorow the parysshe 8d."*

This particular procession of Queen Elizabeth occurred when she was en route from Great Leighs Priory on August the 24th 1561 to Great Hallingbury (see walk 2).

Court cases and their results are a very good source of information on the perceptions of the times. For instance in 1585 Peter Jenkynson and five others were arraigned at the Quarter Sessions for playing unlawful games called 'the bowles' on Sunday at Little Dunmow. Clearly they were expected at Church; as were seven other parties, for in 1595 they also were arraigned for -

> *"not coming to our parish Church of Dunmow for the space*

of one year and for not receiving the sacrament.'

Also in the chronicles of the Quarter Sessions, dated October 13, 1660 is the following:

"Henry Fowler of Great Dunmow husbandman for stealing a horse colour sorrell worth £3 belonging to John Clarke, at Wethersfield. Guilty to be hanged."

In 1642 the 'trained Bands' and 'volunteer Companies' of Dunmow and the surrounding areas attended a meeting [1], the purpose of which was to pass a resolution in support of a petition to Parliament. This petition noted that:

"- his Majestie, served by wicked counsell intends to make war against the Parliament that so to doe is a breach of the trust reposed in him by his people, contrary to his oath, and that Whosoever shall serve or assist him in his warres are trayters to the fundamental laws of the kingdom."

Notwithstanding this the petition then goes on to inform King Charles that:

"With our hands upon our swords, we stand ready at your command... to spend our dearest blood in defence of the lives and liberties of our countrymen, the lawes which are the life of our liberty and peace, and religion more precious than both."

I think the reader will have detected a certain amount of 'double-speak' here that might be considered worthy of George Orwell's 'pigs' (with apologies to Dunmow), as featured in his book '1984' (written in 1949). In fact, in the year of the rebellion (1642), the citizens of Dunmow were staunch Parliamentarians and as such were certainly not on the side of the King. At this time the people concerned had very strong feelings as witnessed by the fact that when they were voting for the resolution to present the petition, it was received with-

> *"universal approbation, by holding up of hands, throwing of hattes and exclamations professing that they held them unnworthy to live, that should dislike it."*

I cannot help wondering how many of the supposed 10,000 people who signed the petition, realised just how carefully it was worded?

Two previous Doctors of Dunmow (of the medical variety), have managed to be included in the historical details of the town. The first of these was a Dr Remington. According to the Journal of the Dunmow and District Historical Society, when King James I of England died in 1624, it was not without suspicion of poison, after a draught of medicine had been prepared by Dr Remington. The second was a Dr John Rayner (or Raynor) 1750-1804, after whom the stretch of water in the town known as 'Doctor's pond' was named. The Rev. W. Langston. Scott was vicar of the parish from 1862 to 1888 and in the Parish Magazine of 1884 he writes:

> *"-It is said that the Lord Maynard of that day and Dr. Rayner and other gentlemen used to play at Bowls at the house, known till quite recently as the 'Bowling Green,' situated,... just above the Pond. He carried out His design, and stocked the Pond with fish, and assumed a kind of guardianship over it."*

Mr. Hastings Worrin writing in reference[7] describes the house as:

> *"-a charming residence standing on the brow of the Downs, which sloped down to the water's side. The garden in which the games of bowls were played was*

House at Doctor's Pond - Great Dunmow known as 'The Bowling Green'

evidently once a part of the green, but it is now walled in."

At the time of writing the house is still called 'The Bowling Green'.

Lionel Lukin

The Doctor's pond is also associated with Lionel Lukin who was born in Dunmow on May 18th 1742, later moving with his family to 'Blatches' in Little Dunmow (see the sketch map of walk 7). He became a fashionable coachbuilder in London and counted the Prince Regent, later George IV, as a personal friend. Lukin was a skilled and inventive craftsman who was also interested in applied mechanics. One of his ancestors was the Elizabethan mathematician Henry Lukyn and on his mother's side he was descended from a family of seafarers, which included an admiral who served in the wars with the Dutch. With such a background it is not surprising that he should be interested in designing a boat which ...

"will be much lighter than any body of water it must displace, so that it will with safety carry more than its common burthen."

Encouraged by the the Prince he applied for a patent on November 2nd 1785, giving details of:

"an improved method of construction of boats...for either sailing or rowing, which will neither overset in violent gales...nor sink by any accident when filled with water."

His patent was subsequently granted and Lukin was able to claim credit for the invention of England's first 'unimmergible boat.' The principles used to construct the boat later became the guide for the design of lifeboats and it is believed that some of his experiments with model boats were carried out on the Doctor's pond. A plaque testifying to this will be found by the roadside at the eastern end of the pond.

The fortunes of natural born inventors are never straightforward and those of Lionel Lukin were no exception. In yet another effort to get his ideas accepted, he was persuaded by the deputy master of Trinity house (a Captain James), to entrust a boat named 'The Experiment' to the care of a pilot from Ramsgate, who had agreed to test it in rough weather off the South coast. The boat behaved so well that it was subsequently taken across the English Channel in weather so bad that other vessels would not venture out of port. Unfortunately for Lukin, such conditions also made it difficult for smugglers to honour the laws of supply and demand and the pilot from Ramsgate succumbed to economic temptation and helped out with the temporary hiatus caused by the bad weather. The ploy was discovered and the boat was impounded and then destroyed in a foreign port by the 'Preventive' men.

Eventually in 1786, Lukin was commissioned by Dr. John Sharp (an archdeacon at Bamburgh on the coast of Northumberland), to equip an existing boat with air tanks for use as a lifeboat. This was successful and in 1790, another boat was converted and Britain's first lifeboat station was established; subsequently to be immortalised by the exploits of Grace Darling and her father, who in 1838, rescued five people from a ship the 'Forfarshire', which had foundered on rocks.

During his lifetime Lukin also designed and produced an adjustable reclining bed for use in hospitals. More details of Lionel Lukin's life can be found in reference[10]. He retired in 1824 to Hythe in Kent where he died in 1834 at the age of 92 years, having been blind for the last 10 years of his life.

The Countess of Warwick.

No history of Dunmow would be complete without mentioning the life and works of Frances Evelyn 'Daisy' Maynard, who married Lord Brooke in 1881, becoming the Countess of Warwick in 1893 and the Lady of the manor of Great Dunmow. Throughout her life she demonstrated her concern for the welfare of the people of Dunmow in a host of practical ways. For 10 years she helped finance a rural school at Bigods, which she referred to as 'My Experiment in Technical Education.' She was in advance of the thinking of her time, in encouraging women to take up managerial positions and one cannot help wondering about the extent of the mental symbiosis which undoubtedly existed between her and H. G. Wells, who was living and writing at 'Easton Glebe' Great Easton between 1912 and 1927. A comprehensive account of her efforts on behalf of the people of Great Dunmow is given in reference[9].

The Clock House

This is the oldest brick house in Dunmow and according to Dorothy Dowsett it was at various times known as Brick House and as Goston Lodge. It was built in 1586 and the facade is nearly all original. The clock is a replica of one on Dover Castle and it is surmounted by an octagonal cupola containing a bell, cast in 1651 by a Brian Eldridge. The shafts of two of the chimneys are octagonal and they also are original.

The house contains two priest's holes, which if only one of them had been in use on Candlemas day in 1601 may have helped save the life of Mrs Ann Line, a 'widowed gentlewoman' who it is believed was the housekeeper at that time. Mrs. Line with her friend Mrs. Gage and a priest, father Page, were just commencing to say mass, when due to a tip off, they were interrupted in their devotions by a set of 'priest hunters'. According to reference [1] the priest escaped

The Clock House - Great Dunmow

but both Mrs. Line and Mrs. Gage were arrested. The latter was subsequently released but Mrs. Line was duly convicted by Lord Chief Justice Popham at the Old Bailey and sentenced to death by hanging. On her journey from Newgate prison to Tyburn she was said to be 'unmoved and of calm countenance.' When the last moments came she said in a loud voice -

> *"I am sentenced to die for harbouring a Catholic priest and as far as I am from repenting I wish with all my soul I could have entertained a thousand."*

Next to be hung were two priests, one of whom (a father Barworth), embraced her dead body saying -

> *"O blessed Mrs. Line, who hast now happily received thy reward, thow hast gone before us, but we shall quickly follow thee to bliss, if it pleases the Almighty."*

A full and almost contemporary account of these grisly happenings can be found in reference[3], which quotes from a recusant manuscript held in the Bodleian Library, Oxford (MSS. Eng. Th. B.1,2).

As an illustration of the way in which bigotry associated with the lack of religious tolerance was nothing if not even handed, it must be mentioned that in 1556, Dunmow had already provided a religious martyr by the name of Thomas Bowyer, a weaver. Under the re-established papist religion of Mary 1st, he would not go to church and after being sent to the prison dungeons at Colchester Castle, he was then condemned by Bishop Bonner of London to be burnt at the stake. This took place at Stratford in East London, along with 10 other men and two women, whose names are recorded on the memorial to the martyrs near St. John's church in Stratford. A plaque to the memory of Thomas Bowyer has been fixed to the bridge now bearing his name approximately 1.6 km (1 mile), from the Clock House on the B184 towards Thaxted.

From 1678 until 1829 the Clock House was occupied by the Beaumont family, with the last two occupants Sir George Howland Beaumont Bart. and his wife, acting as hosts to some of the leading poets and artists of that time. Coleridge stayed with them in 1804 and Wordsworth in 1809 and in those times both men praised the beautiful scenery and quiet serenity of Dunmow. Sir George himself was a poet and he was also a man of great tact. He helped persuade the Government to give to the nation the Angerstein collection, which, with a further gift of 16 of his own paintings, was largely responsible for the inception of the National Gallery in 1824.

The Saracen's Head Hotel.

The Saracen's Head Hotel was a coaching and posting house. Parts of it are 400 years old and in the early part of the 17th century it was owned by a family called Deane, whose son became Lord Mayor of London in 1634. One infamous landlord at the inn had a reputation for also being a smuggler and a highway man, who no doubt being privy to inside information, found himself able to profit from his unsuspecting guests; first as 'mine host' and second in one or other of his other guises. Such despicable behaviour was not uncommon and in 1679 the Privy Council drew up a list of known highwaymen, in which the Boar's Head in Braintree was specifically mentioned as being a haven for thieves and vagabonds [13]. This was clearly typical of those times as illustrated by William Shakespeare in the first part of King Henry IV Part I, written in the year 1597-8. The scene is set for us and for his play, in the yard of an inn with 'gentlemen of the shade.'

CHAMBERLAIN. *"Good morrow , Master Gadshill. It holds current that I told you yesternight:-there's a franklin in the wild of Kent hath brought three hundred marks with* *him in gold: I heard him tell it to one of his company last night at supper; a kind of auditor; one that hath abundance of charge too, God knows what. They are up already, and call for eggs and butter; they will away presently."*

GADSHILL. *"Sirrah, if they meet not with Saint Nicholas' clerks, I'll give thee this neck."*

NOTES [14]

franklin, a small landowner. Originally a franklin was a landowner of free but not noble birth.

Saint Nicholas, "old nick." Thus Saint Nicholas' clerks are thieves.

The Church of Saint Mary The Virgin Great Dunmow.

The church is sited in the Chelmer valley at Church End, grid reference TL 629 229. It is equidistant from the Town and Bigods Hall, grid reference TL 627 246. According to reference[4] Bigods was once a hamlet belonging to the parish of Dunmow and the author of reference[5] quotes W. T. Scott, as conjecturing that the position of the church site was the result of a compromise between the Lord of the Manor of Bigods and the Townsfolk. He adds that Bigods was 'laid to Dunmow' soon after 1200.

However according to reference[8], Roman settlements existed at both Churchend and Great Dunmow and both these settlements were subsequently occupied by Saxons. The authors go on to state that the area at Churchend probably became the principal focus for settlement. The author of reference[5] writes:

"The first Church on the present site was probably built about 1250 though we do not know anything of the names

of the builders."

He also records that substantial rebuilding took place around 1350 and that the doorway of the porch leading into the south aisle of the present church incorporates a beautifully moulded archway, which has been retained from the earlier church, (presumably the one built around 1250). There is evidence of the earlier existence of a church in Dunmow (on an unknown site), because in 1045 a person called 'Thurston' left half a hide of land and a toft (or homestead) to it. Also it is known that a Geoffrey de Dunmow was Rector in 1197.

The Chancel contains an early 16th century iron bound chest which may at one time have been used to hold the church valuables and possibly also the information on births, marriages and deaths commissioned by Thomas Cromwell. Within the communion rails on the floor of the chancel (built in 1322) is an epitaph engraved as follows:

"Mr. Thomas Beaumont fecond fon of Sir Thomas Beaumont of Stowghton-grange in Leicefterfhire, bart. He married Sufannah, daughter of William Oldys, D.D. vicar of Alderbury in Oxfordshire..."

Muilman P. in reference[4] relates the following story about Dr. Oldys:

"He was returning from Oxford, where he had been to admit his fon (to university), and fearing he fhould fall into the hands of the parliament foldiers, ordered his fervant to ride at fome difstance before him, and, if he faw any of them, to drop his handkerchief as a fignal for him to go back to the garrifon of Oxford, or Banbury: the man dropped the handkerchief, which his mafter paffed without feeing. As foon as he perceived the enemy he turned about, but his malignant horfe would not leave his road, fo he was fhot through the back."

It is salutary to note that Mr. Muilman (Gentlman), does not record what became of the servant.

In pre-reformation days the Guild chapel was located over the South entrance of the church and the gallery is believed to have been an extension to it. The gallery later served as a family pew for the occupants of the Manor of Newton Hall.

Details of Walk 8

Map required:
Ordnance Survey Pathfinder No. 1075 (TL 62/72) Great Dunmow and Braintree 1:25 000.
Starting and finishing point:
High Street car park (off White Street) adjacent to the Co-operative supermarket.
Grid reference TL 6285 2192.
Distance covered:
6.4 km (4 miles).
Duration of walk:
2 h 30 min. including a 30 minute break:
Condition of terrain:
Generally firm and relatively smooth. Those sections of the walk marked A-B and C-D Are not well maintained. In the section C-D it is suggested that walkers follow the power lines to the boundary of the wood.

Places of Refreshment:
In Great Dunmow there is a wide choice of establishments offering refreshment.

Leave the car park by returning to the High Street. This part of the High Street is part of the original Roman road (see sketch map), which came into the town from the north west. Turn left and walk towards the War Memorial turning right into New Street. This was a medieval development and was 'new' in 1527. Approximately 70 m along the street turn right moving in a westerly direction and at the end of the sunken allotments bear right. This path is almost co-linear

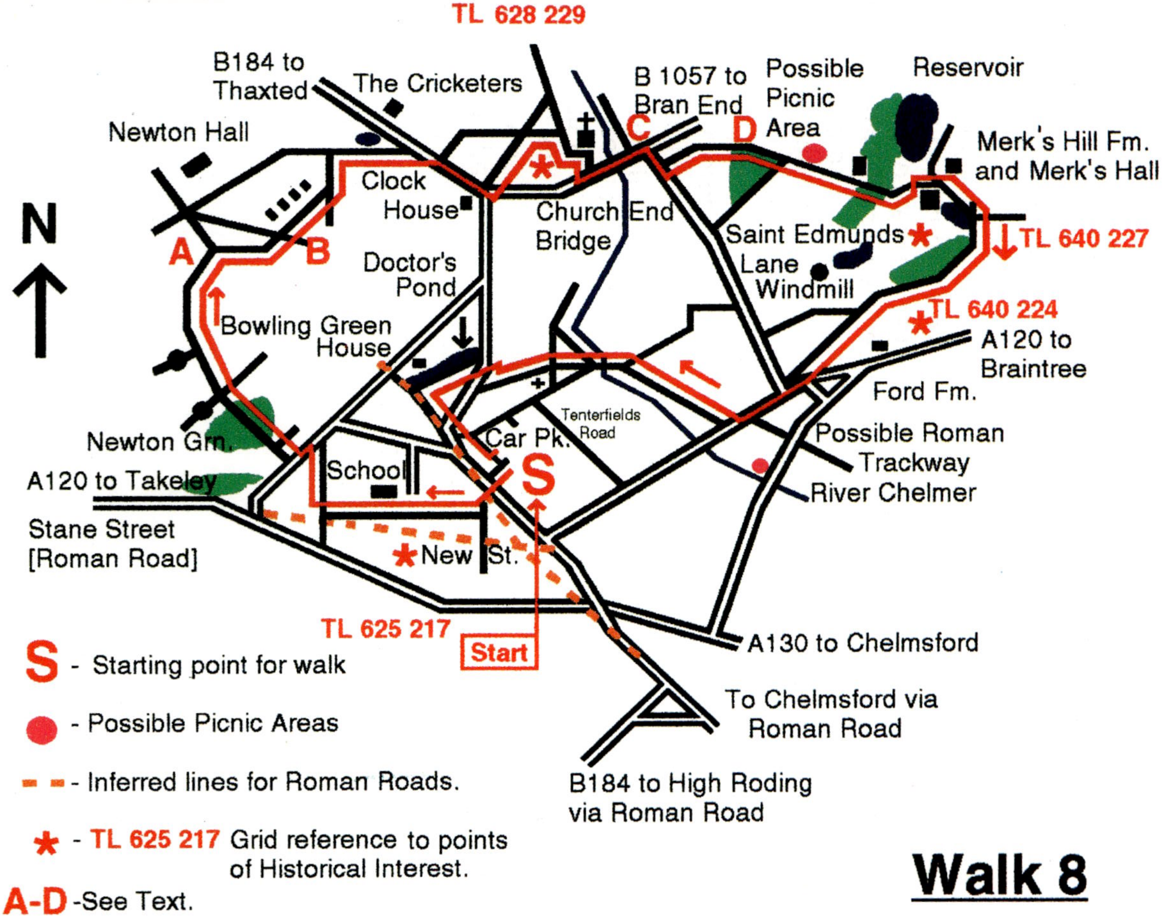
TL 628 229
B184 to Thaxted
The Cricketers
B 1057 to Bran End
Possible Picnic Area
Reservoir
Newton Hall
Clock House
Church End
Bridge
Merk's Hill Fm. and Merk's Hall
Saint Edmunds
Lane Windmill
TL 640 227
A
B
C
D
Doctor's Pond
Bowling Green House
TL 640 224
A120 to Braintree
Ford Fm.
Tenterfields Road
Car Pk.
Possible Roman Trackway
River Chelmer
Newton Grn.
A120 to Takeley
School
S
Stane Street [Roman Road]
New St.
TL 625 217
Start
A130 to Chelmsford
To Chelmsford via Roman Road
B184 to High Roding via Roman Road
N
S - Starting point for walk
- Possible Picnic Areas
- Inferred lines for Roman Roads.
* - TL 625 217 Grid reference to points of Historical Interest.
A-D -See Text.

Walk 8

with the inferred course of the Roman Road (shown dotted on the sketch map) and it passes through the centre of the Roman settlement of that time [11]. Roman cemetries are known to have existed on the north and south sides of the path and Roman and Saxon artefacts have been unearthed in this area.

According to the Archaeology Department of Essex County Council, the area around grid reference TL 625 217 (see sketch map), has yielded ... 'a scatter of flint gritted prehistoric pottery indicating spasmodic occupation.' Also ... 'Occupation of the site by the Romans occurred from the first century on what was apparently virgin ground, until the fourth or fifth centuries, after which the site was used for agricultural purposes with an interlude occurring in the mid Saxon period, between the seventh and the ninth centuries.'

The walk may be continued by turning right into High Stile, left into the Stortford Road and then right again into Green Lane leading onto Newton Green. The footpath leaves the Green from its north western edge, crossing some partially finished roadworks and continues in the direction of Newton Hall, one of the Manors of Dunmow. The Hall is now private property and it can only be seen from the footpath in wintertime when the trees surrounding it have lost their leaves. Before the Domesday survey, in the reign of Edward the Confessor (so nicknamed because of his piety), it was owned by a Saxon called Ururic Cauna, who was later dispossessed by William the Conqueror who subsequently gave it to Geffrey de Magnaville (Mandeville).

On reaching the B184 road to Thaxted, walkers should turn right towards Dunmow. At the tee junction they will then be able to view the exterior of Clock House, before taking the footpath leading in a north easterly direction to Churchend. East of the footpath, at grid reference TL 628 229, cropmarks have been photographed of three 10 m square ditched enclosures and a ring ditch, [12]. These are believed to be barrows of the Iron Age, characteristic of the Arras culture, which are also to be found in Yorkshire and at Mucking in Essex.

The present bridge over the river Chelmer was built in 1882. The ground beneath it consisted of 1.2 m (4 feet) of topsoil, resting on a bed of peat 2.4 m (8 feet) thick. In order to reach firm ground, a total of 50 piles each 6 m (20 feet) long were required. The construction costs were borne by The quarter sessions at Chelmsford, the Highways department of Dunmow, Lady Brooke, the Rev. J H Hallet and the citizens of Dunwow. At the opening ceremony the last stone was laid (no doubt graciously), by Lady Brooke.

The walk continues towards Merks Hall. The name originates from Adelop de Merc who held the manor of Merks in 1086. The previous owner was a Saxon freeman called Edmar, who (like Ururic at Newton Hall), was of course dispossessed and his property given to the 'new' Norman owner. In 1760 at a point south west of Merks Hall, at grid reference TL 640 227 (see sketch map), gravel diggers found a probable grave group consisting of a dozen small urns and copper and brass coins, among which was a Trajan and Antoninus Pius.

The footpath leading south west from the pond at Merks Hall is considered by C. J. Going [12], to be a possible Roman trackway. South of this trackway at grid reference TL 640 224, extensive cropmarks show a 40 m square enclosure having rounded corners, divided into western and eastern halves. Together with the previous find and other faint cropmarks, the same reference suggests the previous existence of a farmstead or villa, having possible Iron Age origins.

The walk continues into Stane Street passing St. Edmund's Lane and taking the next footpath leading in a north westerly direction running parallel with and eventually crossing the River Chelmer. The route joins the Thaxted road near the Doctor's pond, via 'Knight's Way'. On the north side of the pond behind and above the willow tree is the house referred to as 'The Bowling Green'. The Market Place may be approached via Star Lane (once called Tanner's Lane), the route of which lies along the old Roman road which entered

Dunmow from the north west skirting the western side of the pond.

On the west side of the Market Place Luckin's grocery shop was sited. It was founded by Samuel Luckin in 1859, but became an economic victim of two large multiple stores, finally closing in June 1997, still with the original shop front and most of the original interior fittings. Could the name of Luckin be associated with that of Henry Lukyn and Lionel Lukin? I have no doubt the answer could be found by those interested in researching family trees.

The old Town Hall is now occupied by a well established firm of estate agents and auctioneers and this is positioned on the east side of the tee junction opposite the Saracen's Head Hotel. It was originally built circa 1565. Over the years changes have been made and the upper storey has been rebuilt.

To return to the car park leave Market Place by turning left into the High Street, continuing past the pump and then turning left into White Street.

References

1 Dowsett Dorothy C. Dunmow Through the Ages.

2 Morant Rev. Philip. The History and Antiquities of the County of Essex.

3 Journal of the Dunmow and District Historical Society. Folio 14 page 107, Shanahan D 'Petticoats on the Gallows', box file in Dunmow library.

4 Muilman P. History of Essex by a Gentleman 1769.

5 The Parish Church of St. Mary the Virgin Great Dunmow a brief history and guide. Box D3 Essex Record Office.

6 Kelly's Directory of Essex 1937.

7 Hastings Worrin. Dunmow and Doctors, the Essex Review vol. 20 1911.

8 Eddy M.R. and Petchey M.R. Historic Towns in Essex, published by Essex County Council, Planning Department.

9 The Dunmow Centenary Book 1894-1994. Published by The Dunmow Historical and Literary Society, 18 Jubilee Court, Great Dunmow, Essex CM6 1DY.

10 Whitnall F.G. `Thousands owe their lives to an Essex man's invention.' Essex Countryside October 1966.

11 Excavations at Great Dunmow 1988. East Anglian Archaeology, Chelmsford Archaeology Trust Rep. No. 7 figure 64. Archaeology Section ECC Planning Dept.

12 Going C.J. An Archaeological Gazeteer of Dunmow.

13 Gibbs Barry. Medieval Transport. Lecture given on Wed. 14th of May 1997 in the Chapter House of Chelmsford Cathedral.

14 Carrington Norman T. Notes on chosen English Texts. Publisher James Brodie Ltd. Bath, Somerset.

The Walthams

Walk 9

THE Saxon word for wood was 'wald' and 'ham' denoted a small settlement or village so that 'Waldham' (Waltham) meant a settlement in the wood. Philip Morant has been referred to as 'The historian of Essex' and he spent the years from 1722 to 1732 as a Curate in the church of St. Mary and St. Lawrence at Great Waltham; which may account (in part), for the extensive chronicling given to this parish in his book 'Histories and Antiquities of the County of Essex'. The information used by Morant was collected over a period of at least 20 years by five different men, none of whom managed to go to print before they died. Morant's information showed that the land around Great Waltham was in Saxon times owned by Asgar (Oscar) and Uluuin and at the time of the General Survey (Domesday), that this area, together with 39 other Lordships in the County of Essex, belonged to Geffrey de Magna villa or Mandeville.

The area was divided into seven 'maners', one of which was the 'maner' of Waltham-bury which included the church at Great Waltham. According to Phillips and Bazett who have written an informative and very readable account of the history pertaining to both Great and Little Waltham [1], Afgar lived at Walthambury before his lands and house were taken by the Normans and given to Geffrey de Mandeville the 1st. His grandson, Geffrey de Mandeville the 2nd, was the founder of Walden Abbey at Saffron Walden, where the Mandevilles had their family seat and where the rights of advowson for the church of Great Waltham were vested. He was given custody of the Tower of London and he had also been given leave to carry out building work at both Pleshey castle and at Saffron Walden. He married Rohesia (sometimes referred to as Poesia) a daughter of Alberic de Vere of Hedingham Castle, whose image was the subject chosen by Lord Tennyson to be immortalised as 'the haughty Lady Vere de Vere'. This lady has also been mentioned in connection with the origin of the town name of Royston (see walk 3).

There is a rather gruesome story about the death of Geffrey de Mandeville the 2nd. King Stephen was the grandson of William the Conqueror and he reigned from 1135-54, having seized the throne from Matilda the daughter of Henry I. When she invaded England in 1139, Civil War resulted and Geffrey the 2nd took the side of Matilda against the King. The King reacted by confiscating his Estates and by relieving him of the custody of the Tower. At this stage Geffrey felt it necessary to sack Romsey and generally to 'lay waste' to the countryside, for which acts he was excommunicated.

Later Geffrey while besieging Stephen at Burwell castle was killed 'because he had just put off his helmet for coolness'[1]. Because of the excommunication his burial could not take place in hallowed ground, so that the monks of Saffron Walden had a problem; ever resourceful, they salted his body, wrapped it in a hide, sealed it in a lead container and hung it in a garden! Clearly such a solution of 'pickling him in a pipe'could not in any way be considered as suitable for the long term, so the Pope was approached and by dispensation, his remains were allowed to be buried in The Temple Church in London, where his bomb damaged effigy can still be seen today.

One of the subsequent holders of the 'maner' of Waltham-bury was Eleanore of Pleshey castle, who lost her husband, Thomas of Woodstock - Duke of Gloucester in suspicious circumstances, after he had been tricked into going to Calais by supporters of Richard II and, more details of this are given under walk 1. At the time of the Dissolution of the Monasteries the manor of Waltham-bury was owned by Lord

Richard Rich, who later passed the Lordship on to Sir Thomas Pope, who gave both the Rectory and the Vicarage to Trinity College Oxford, with whom the church is still associated.

The Black Death of 1348 removed 45% of the working (and tithing) men from Great Waltham, with the effect that the labourer discovered he was indeed 'worthy of his hire' and this must have been one of those rare periods when the potential employers (the Lords of the Manor), felt threatened by the system. So much so that in 1351, using Civil Law they set about specifying the maximum wage that could be offered in case the workers ultimately demanded more! So great was the imbalance in market forces that certain landowners did in fact offer wages above the recommended maximum specified and in the following year, in Great Waltham, this resulted in their being fined the sum of nine pounds! The Law also allowed for fines to be levied on the labourers if they demanded payment above the maximum allowed.

During 1970-71 archaeologists carried out excavations in the area of Ash Tree corner along the line of what was then the proposed route of the Little Waltham bypass and the subsequent findings have been recorded in detail by Paul J. Drury [2]. He notes that there was evidence of occupation, (which was not necessarily continuous), from the Neolithic period onwards, within a radius of about 500m from the point at which the present bye-pass crosses the river. An analysis of the worked flints which were found, showed that some were Mesolithic in orign, while others were typical of Neolithic and Bronze Age periods. Also unearthed was a hearth and gulley containing some pottery which was radiocarbon dated to 3170 ± 130 BC., (equivalent to a calendar date of 3960 ± 130 BC.).

Evidence of the existence of 15 pre Belgic Iron Age huts arranged in the configuration of an open settlement, were dated from circa mid 3rd to the late 2nd centuries BC. In addition to this, evidence of at least two pallisaded circular huts was also found, which formed an enclosed settlement, dating from the late 2nd to the mid 1st centuries BC. Also the post holes for a single hut with associated pottery were unearthed and dated circa the 3rd quarter of the 1st century BC.

Other discoveries adjacent to the area together with previously attested finds indicated Romano-British occupation and a single croft from the 12th century was found at the 'old' Ash Tree corner road junction. Late and post-medieval periods were represented by evidence of pits for the extraction of gravel and chalk and boulder clay. Drury states: 'that in the Roman period there was a concentration of activity around the road junction at Waltham'. He goes on to suggest that this may have included two or three farms with houses for their workers and for a small number of artisans.

In appendix I of Mr Drury's archaeological report Ms D.Gay Wilson of the School of Botany at Cambridge University, reports on an analysis of Iron Age and Roman plant remains. One soil sample taken from a Roman well, yielded a relatively high proportion of stinging nettles of the variety 'Urtica dioica', a plant which is characterised by having small easily detachable needles lining the underside of each leaf. All walkers (particularly those who wear shorts), will have experienced the effects of making contact with this plant and the appendix to the report contains an interestingly apochryphal story which credits Roman soldiers with having introduced the nettle into this and other 'cold' countries.

The story suggests that the nettles were needed and subsequently used by these soldiers from a 'walm' Mediterranean climate, to help restore the circulation of blood to their bodily extremities by rubbing them into the afflicted parts! In fact Ms Wilson points out that the stinging nettle was indigenous to Britain before the Romans arrived. She also states that the Roman soldiers wore breeches in 'cold' countries and reminds us that it was not unknown for them to use warm (Roman) baths to combat the cold! An additional entry notes that in the Satyricon of Petronius (written in the 1st century AD.); there is a report of a man's potency being restored, by first annointing him with ground pepper, ground nettle seed and oil and then beating him with nettles! Ms Wilson also mentions that as late as the middle of the 19th century, arthritic or paralytic patients were beaten with nettles with the object of effecting a cure; clearly desperate conditions required desperate deeds!

The Church of St. Mary and St. Lawrence Great Waltham

The nave of the church is Norman, built between 1080 and 1100 and it is possible that it replaced a Saxon church that may have existed on the same site. The roof of the nave is about 485 years old and in common with many other churches Roman bricks have been used to help in the building. It is likely that these bricks came from the site of a Roman villa approximately 2 km south west of Ash Tree corner, at grid reference TL 693 111.

There is an odd legend about monks starting to build the present church on Church Field. This field now encompasses the cricket pitch and it is codified on the Tithe Map of 1839 with the number 959. It is good arable land and it has a much larger area than the ground on which the present church stands. Traditionally churches have always been built on poor land, such as that which could only support sheep and goats and in this case, it seems that as fast as the monks began to raise stones on Church Field, they were mysteriously removed to the present site. Legend has it that this could only have been the work of the Devil, who in this instance seems to have been firmly on the side of those who worked the land and who relied upon it for their subsistence.

In the middle of the 14th century the Warner family added the south aisle of the nave where their Family Crest may be seen carved in the roof timbers. Curiously however several monuments to the family are known to have disappeared during church restorations [3]. The north aisle was added in the 19th century. Some of the pews at the western end of the nave are reputed to be among the oldest in the country, dating from about 1420. Closer inspection will reveal the original marks of the adze used to make the horizontal and vertical surfaces tolerably smooth and plane, but alas, in spite of the craftsmen's skill, I can personally guarantee that the pews will be judged as being uncomfortable when used for prolonged periods! Clearly I (and others), are missing something, - like properly upholstered and anatomically shaped seats?

The superbly renovated marble and alabaster monument now situated in the north east corner of the nave is of Sir Richard Everard and his wife Ann. He died in 1614 and his wife who was a cousin of Oliver Cromwell died in 1609. Interestingly the sculptor of the monument has departed from the tradition of presenting the figures supine; Sir Richard does appear to be at ease, but it has to be said that his wife's position, with her head being supported by just three fingers, does not seem to be naturally sustainable for anything other than a short period!

The church retains the oldest piece of plate in Essex [3]; this is a pre-Reformation Patten dating from 1521, which survived the confiscation of church property by King Henry VIII which took place in 1547. Later, this and other plate dated 1632, also survived the call for actual liquidation, with no thanks to those responsible for financing the Cromwellian army. Richard Everard (a descendant of Sir Anthony Everard), was on the side of the King, whilst his two daughters were for the Parliamentary cause. Could there have been some 'inside' information which prompted Richard to arrange for the plate to be secreted away from where others would expect to find it? Whatever happened, the outcome has preserved the continuity of ownership of most of the valuables to this day.

On the wall at the south side of the nave are two very good examples of 'eulogies' as practised in the 18th century.

Monument to Sir Richard Everard and
his wife Anne - Great Waltham Church

One of these is to Peter Curgenven a merchant who:

"Preparing after a 25 years absence to return to his native country he unfortunately fell into the hands of CONNAJEE ANGRIA admiral to the SOU RAJAH then at war with the ENGLISH at Bombay and remained in a miferable captivity about 5 years during which he behaved with an unparalleled Patience Generofity and Greatnefs of mind not only comforting affifting and supporting his fellow sufferers but even refufing his own deliverance without that of his Companions in Mifery. At laft having freed him felf and the reft by his own induftry and Management He embarked for ENGLAND in hopes of fitting down in quiet and enjoying the fruits of his labours."

Much more suffering (borne in an exemplary fashion) was to come:

"But fee the uncertainty of all things here below. Juft before his landing a violent fit of the cramp feizing his Thigh and burfting the veins tho the effects were hardly difernable yet was he forc'd foon after his arrival at LONDON to have his thigh firft laid open and then cut off almoft clofe to his body. Scarce ever was the like operation perform'd. Never ever undergone with more refolution and Firmnefs without so much as a groan or the leaft Motion to exprefs his anguish."

In his time it was frequently the case that one could expect to die after a 'successful' operation; the carver in stone goes on to record that:

"He outlive'd this operation 12 days when the wound bleeding afrefh he refign'd his laft breath with a surprizing sedatenefs and unconcern at leaving this world being fully perfuaded he was going to exchange his perifhable for everlafting riches. 1729 47th year."

The other eulogy also carved in stone is to Hugh Everard an ex pupil of Felsted school, who was wrecked on the Goodwin sands in 1703. His exploits are chronicled in true 'Boy's Own' manner and need to be read to be believed!

The door to the vestry is thought to have once been an external door and it still carries the door knocker, which once grasped would ensure that the sanctuary of the church would automatically be granted to any fugitive. The church has eight bells, the oldest of which was cast in 1336 and the newest in 1796. The tenor bell was cast in 1663 and has a mass of 1,270 kg and a diameter of 1.32 m.

On the south eastern corner of the church wall two mass sundials have been fixed one above the other. On the south side of the churchyard are a group of cottages and the coaching Inn; all of which at one time had their frontages facing the church, so that it is logical to conclude that the trackway would at that time have passed between the church and the front of the cottages. The stables belonging to the coaching Inn together with the cottages in which the ostlers lived, were on the other side of the present road [4].

The present lychgate at the western side of the churchyard is built on the site of the original Guildhall which was demolished in the late 18th or early 19th centuries.

The Manor of Langleys

From the time of the reign of King John from 1199 to that of Edward III (1327-77), a family having the name of Mareskull owned the manor of Marshalls or Mariskalls. In 1421 ownership then passed to John Langeley and the manor then became known as Langleys [5].

Later the Estate was divided into two parts, one part being sold to Thomas Cornish and his wife Idonea and the other part to John Slixton and his wife Joan. In 1515 the grandson of Thomas Cornish (John Cornish), passed his part of the Estate to Thomas Everard, who had married their daughter and heir. In 1529 the other half of the property was passed from John Slixton and his son John, to Richard Everard and the whole estate was then owned by the Everard family until 1710, when it was sold to Samuel Tufnell by Dame Mary Everard, widow of Sir Hugh Everard, whose eldest son also called Richard Everard, subsequently went to the North American Colonies becoming Governor of North Carolina in 1724 [1,5].

After purchasing Langleys Samuel Tufnell spent the next ten years rebuilding and renovating the house. He added the second floor and raised the ceiling of the Saloon, making a cube-shaped space. The ceilings of two of the rooms dating from the time of James I (1603-25), contained fine examples of English plasterwork and at that time these were retained in the north wing of the 'new' building [6]. Successive owners have all added to and modified the house, so making it possible for the building to be used as a private dwelling.

The penultimate owner of Langleys was Mr John Jolliffe Tufnell, the fourth member of the family to bear that name. On his return from serving in the last war, he realised that the kitchen and servants' quarters would require a 'change of use' and he then embarked on a series of repairs and modifications designed to satisfy modern-day requirements. This involved the demolition of extensive Victorian buildings which included a large 'Winter' garden in which much of the glass had been broken during air raids. In 1969 the House and Estate were passed by Mr Tufnell to his neice Mrs David Micklem and she and her family have now been in residence there since 1971. Mr Tufnell died in 1990 [7].

It is interesting to note that according to an old map held by Mrs Micklem at Langleys, the road from Chelmsford to Dunmow ran in a north westerly direction across the Park, between the North and South Lodges and it is thought that the present footpath more or less follows the old road [1]. The earlier road was closed in the 18th century by the then owner of Langleys and all the traffic was forced to take the 'back road' (now the main road), through the village and past the church.

The mill at Langleys is no longer in existence, but in the

Langleys - Great Waltham

past it had been known as Marshall's or Mascall's mill and it was in operation when Edward the Confessor was on the throne. It is not known when it stopped functioning, however the 'Mill Room' can still be seen and around 1900 it was used as a village hall, when harvest suppers were organised. Miss Olive Tufnell had the idea of teaching the intricate art of lacemaking to a young physically handicapped girl, in order to give her a new interest. This kind act was well received and the venture grew to include more handicapped children and some adults, so that at one time a class of 40-50 people was held on a Saturday on a regular weekly basis in the Mill Room [8]. The black rabbits in the park are the results of another project carried out by Miss Olive Tufnell early on in the 1900's.

The grounds around the House take the form of parkland, but in earlier times herds of deer were farmed and they once supplied meat for both those who owned the herd and for those who poached them. James I allowed landowners some defrayment of taxes if deer were kept mainly for 'sport' and the park at Langleys was stocked with fallow deer until 1939-40. Many properties were let by the Lord of the Manor for a small payment together with the stipulation that the lessee should also 'furnish him with one pound of pepper yearly'. According to an old recipe, this amount of pepper was just sufficient to help condition and preserve one red deer[1].

Little Waltham

In Saxon times the district was in the possession of Lefstan an abbott of St. Edmunsbury (Bury St. Edmunds). However at the time of the Domesday Survey the area is listed as belonging to Eustace Earl of Bologne (Boulogne). A subsequent owner of Little Waltham was Sir John de Clifton who was called to Parliament from 1377 to 1388 and who, wishing to undertake a mission to the Holy Land, sold or mortgaged his estate to Richard de Waltham, only to depart this life on the island of Rhodes. Other subsequent owners were Thomas Mildmay of Moulsham 1447 and the Luckyn family in 1625 [9].

St. Martin's Church Little Waltham

The nave of the church was built early in the 12th century and still has a south doorway of Norman origin, together with a Norman window high up just above the entrance. The combination of thick walls, high windows and extremely well made wooden doors is plainly designed to keep the attentions of any unwanted marauding mercenaries away from those taking refuge in the church.

A good example of the work of a carpenter of the time of the late 13th to early 14th centuries, can be seen in the form of a sycamore chest having two compartments hewn out of a single piece of wood. The chest contained the records of the church and it is convincingly bound with wrought iron bands, which also make provision for two locks and four padlocks. The keys for these were reputed to have been held by the rector and five other persons, so that access to the contents of the box was clearly not meant to be readily obtainable.

According to Benson and Chapman [9], In early times the nave was quite open and free of pews and worshippers stood or knelt to pray on the bare paved floor. Only the weak or aged were allowed to be seated on settles around the walls, hence the saying – 'the weakest to the wall'.

In the late 19th century there was a great deal of poverty which forced people to try and be self sufficient. Access to land which would support pigs and chickens and which could also be used to grow vegetables, became all important and in the Walthams, those without gardens were allowed access to an allotment. A cautionary tale indicative of the extreme class distinction of the time, has it that in 1887 a Reverend Tweed felt it necessary to deprive a man of his allotment, because his wife did not curtsy to Mrs Tweed! There must have been some very good reasons why one woman would not comply with the expected social mores to another and why the rector felt he had to react in such an extreme fashion!

Details of Walk 9

Map required:
Ordnance Survey Pathfinder Map No. 1098 (TL 61/71) Great and Little Waltham
1:25 000.
Starting and finishing point:
Great Waltham village hall car park, grid reference TL 695 133.

The prescribed walk following the red arrows.
Distance covered:
10.1 km (6.25 miles).
Duration of walk:
3 h 45 min. including a 30 minute break:
Condition of terrain:
Generally firm and relatively smooth.

The shorter walk following the green arrows.
Distance covered:
7.25 km (4.5 miles).
Duration of walk:
2 h 45 min. including a 30 minute break:
Condition of terrain:
Generally firm and relatively smooth.

Places of Refreshment:
In Great Waltham there are three public houses (two of which have restaurants) and in Little Waltham there are two public houses, both of which provide food.

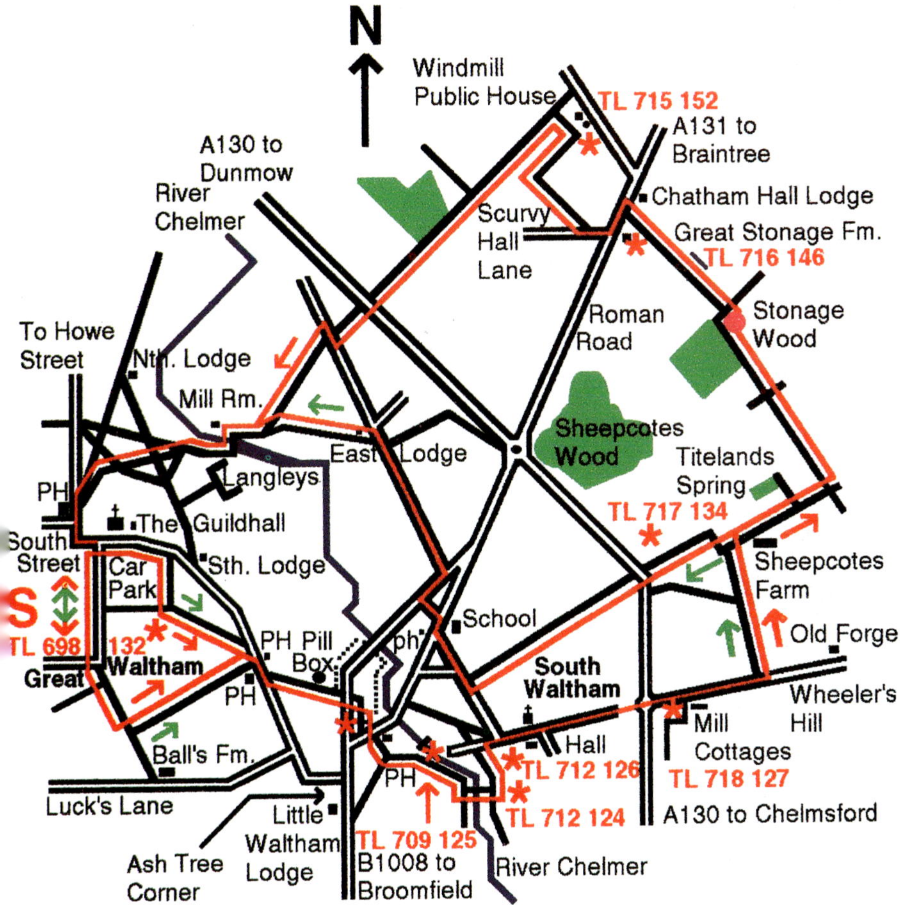

● - Possible picnic area

* - TL 698 132 Grid reference for point of Historical interest.

S - Starting point for both walks. For the prescribed walk follow the red arrows. For the shorter walk follow the green arrows.

Walk 9

In Chatham Green there is one public house with a restaurant.

At the start, walkers may choose to leave Great Waltham and get some good views across open farmland, by first walking in a southerly direction towards the bend of South Street and then taking the footpath shown on the sketch map. This path reachs the main Chelmsford Road, at a point approximately half way between the two public houses. At this point walkers should turn right before taking the path opposite to the Windmill public house.

Alternatively the walk may be commenced from the car park exit by turning to the north towards the main road and Great Waltham church. For those who wish to visit the church it is open every Saturday both morning and afternoon from 10.30 until noon and from 2.30 until 3.30.

Turn right at the main road and on the east side of the church is a house which was in existence in 1577 when it was occupied by an Edward Burde and was known as 'Baddinghams'. The main external feature dominating all sides of the property is the eight Tudor chimneys which are arranged in four groups of two. Interestingly when planning the decorative finials, the original designer has chosen to present us with what many would now regard as a timeless and rather un-subtle basic joke, in that the decorations on all of the eight chimneys are phallic. It is understood that this rather startling form of decoration was not unusual at the time and that it was believed to act as a talisman against evil influences. As a matter of interest the Parsonage in Wicken Road in Newport also has the finials of its chimneys decorated in a similar manner.

The front elevation of the house once contained a general store known as 'Brown's' and also the Post Office, which was sited separately on the right hand side. Mr.J.J.Tufnell bought the house in the 1960's and built a new village shop, the Walthambury Stores in Barrack Lane. He then converted the house for use as a dwelling place and lived in it for some years having re-named it 'The Guildhall'.

Tudor chimneys at The Guildhall [Baddinghams] -Great Waltham

Walkers should continue eastwards along the main road towards the South Lodge, which in the 18th century marked the turning point for the main road as it crossed Langley's Park in the direction of Dunmow. At this point it is possible to continue along the main Great Waltham road to the Windmill public house, or to take the signposted footpath just past Hatchfields on the right to Minnow End.

The footpath passes close to grid reference TL 6980 1320 in 'Dickeymoors', where excavations revealed a possible gravel pit of late Roman date, which has yielded pottery from the fifth century onwards [10]. Rejoining the main road turn right and after deliberately passing two public houses, take the signposted footpath leading across the field in a south easterly direction towards the Little Waltham bypass, passing just to the right of the concrete pillbox and continuing on towards the main road. This stretch of road passes over the site of the archaeological dig carried out by P Drury and, as an alternative to crossing at this point and negotiating the traffic, parts of the site can be walked by following the dotted lines (shown on the sketch map), passing under the road bridge which crosses the river Chelmer. It should be mentioned that this particular part of the walk contains an abundance of the variety of stinging nettles of the variety 'Urtica dioica' which have been mentioned earlier in the text and it follows that some walkers might find it preferable to negotiate the traffic!

The next bridge over the Chelmer is located in 'The Street' at Little Waltham and it is called 'Winkford Bridge', after a Saxon called 'Wineca', who lent his name to a ford where the bridge now stands. Walkers should pass through the car park of the Bell public house emerging via the footpath on the right hand side, which after joining with another path leads towards the river Chelmer and the site of the now demolished Little Waltham Mill. A great deal of information on the past owners and the operation of this mill is given by Phillips and Bazett [1] and Kenneth Farries [11]. The latter pinpoints the old site at grid reference TL 709 125.

The Guildhall [Baddinghams] - Great Waltham

At grid reference TL 712 124 shown on the sketch map Saxo-Norman pottery has been dug out of the sides of an old gravel pit and the records kept by the archaeology section of Essex County Council Planning Department, refer to a possible Anglo-Saxon settlement site which is located approximately 35 m to the east of the junction of the footpaths. Continuing northwards, turn right towards Little Waltham church where at grid reference TL 712 126 near to Little Waltham Hall, shards of pottery of possible Iron age origin (now in the custody of the Colchester museum), have been collected from trenches dug by builders.

At the next point of interest grid reference TL 718 127 on Wheeler's Hill, a post mill once stood at the point where the footpath going south from the road, exhibits a 'dog's leg' [11]. In 1770 the mill was operated by Thomas Millbank and later in 1839 it was owned by a Charles Skill who also owned the mill at Little Waltham [1]. Two or three mill cottages can be seen adjacent to the site. The walk turns northwards from Wheeler's Hill towards Sheepcotes Farm, at which point those wishing to take the shorter route should turn westwards and continue by following the green arrows as shown on the sketch map and those continuing on the prescribed walk should turn eastwards, passing through the farm on their way to Stonage Wood.

Grid reference TL 7172 1340 gives the position at which in 1901 a hoard of about 180 Roman coins dating to the latter half of the third century was found by two men digging for gravel. The coins were together at a depth of 1 m and included those of the Emperors Postumus and Victorinus. They represent a few of the many thousands of such coins that have been found in the country. Some of the coins are held at Chelmsford Museum and the rest, which are held at Langleys, are in relatively poor condition. Further references to this can be found in reference[2].

Great Stonage Farm at grid reference TL 716 146 , has a 15th century house together with the remains of a moat. In 1337 it was known to have been the home of John 'atte

Stonhach' and it is referred to again in 1517 as 'Stonehache' [10]. Walkers will emerge onto the old Roman road, when they should turn left and then right, crossing the present road at Scurvy Hall Lane. The sign posted footpath to the right then connects with the Essex Way.

If the need for refreshment is felt this can be obtained by approaching the adjacent public house (also known as 'The Windmill' at TL 715 152), where the lower part of a post mill first mentioned in 1829 can now be seen, having been converted into residential accommodation as part of the Windmill public house. The ground floor of the present structure has served over the years variously as a pig sty, a dance floor and a beer saloon [11].

Chatham Hall was one of the seven manors of Great Waltham and at Domesday it was referred to as Cetham. 'Cet' is Romano-British for wood and 'ham' is Saxon for a dwelling place. Some Lords of the manor were entitled to hold their own courts and at the time these were referred to as 'Court Leets' and both Chatham Hall and Little Waltham had this privilege.

By rejoining the Essex Way and walking in a south westerly direction towards Langleys, it will be seen that the paths of both walks converge, leading on towards the Old Mill Room at Langleys. Kenneth Farries gives the site of the Old Mill as being at grid reference TL 698 138. The walk continues via the private driveways and footpaths on the Estate to the main road leading back to Great Waltham.

Just after leaving the Park walkers should look out for the sunken garden located on the western side of the main road. Originally this was leased from the Estate at Langleys 'for the use of the villagers and passers by' and it has been magnanimously maintained for many years, by the voluntary efforts of a group of people headed by Mrs Eve Coulson. The owner of the land is now Mr. Alexander Micklem of Chatham Hall.

Just before returning to the car park the route passes Barrack Lane, which was so called because of the billeting of soldiers who in 1803 were destined to serve in the Napoleonic Wars.

References

1 Phillips and Bazett. Ages in the Making, A History of Two Essex Villages.

2 Drury P.J. Excavations at Little Waltham 1970-71, Report 1 of the Chelmsford Excavation Committee, CBA Research Report 26.

3 Jukes B.W. Reverend. Great Waltham Parish Church Through the Centuries. Chelmsford Record Office Box W3.

4 Information given by Mrs. Eve Coulson of Great Waltham.

5 Philip Morant Reverend. History and Antiquities of the County of Essex 1768.

6 Whiteman G.W. Some famous English Country Homes from the time of Henry VIII to the Regency, 'Langleys', 1951.

7 Verbal and documentary information given by Mrs David Micklem of Langleys.

8 Smith C. Fell. Lace-making at Great Waltham, the Essex Review 1905.

9 Benson T.N. Chapman T.A. A Short History of Little Waltham. Coronation 1953.

10 The Archaeology Section, Essex County Council Planning Department, County Hall, Chelmsford. Archaeology Assistant Ms Alison Bennett.

11 Kenneth George Farries. Essex Windmills, Millers and Millwrights five vols. Dewey 621.45.

Coggeshall

Walk 10

THE Roman road Stane Street (meaning a paved way), skirts the southern side of the town and connects Colchester (Camulodonum), with St. Albans (Verulamium). Local lore has it that in 61 A.D. Queen Boadicea travelled along this road at the head of the Iceni tribe, on her way to rout the Romans at Colchester. The modern road is called East Street (once known as Gallow's Street); it leads into West Street and both roads are built on top of the ancient trackway. Many Roman artefacts have been found in the area north of Stane Street, suggesting that a Roman station was nearby. Coins dating from 31 B.C. to 395 A.D. have been found in the area.

The eminent historian Reverend Philip Morant records the finding by others of an arched vault of brick containing a burial urn and some sacrificial dishes near to the site of a Roman villa, adjoining a road leading in to the town called 'Coccill-Way'. Could either (or both), East and West Streets have once been named 'Coccil-Way'? The underside of one sacrificial dish carried the inscription 'COCCILIM'. This is thought to represent 'Coccil-li.m.' or 'Coccilli Manibus' ie 'to the manes (manors) of Coccillus', whom Morant presumes to have been the Roman Lord of the town and from whom he suggests its name is derived. Dr.P.H.Reaney in 'The Place Names of Essex' [1] records that Coggeshall was probably once known as 'Cocc's nook' and he then refers to the way in which at the time of the Norman Conquest it was common for the letter 'c' to be replaced with the French 'g', which could account for the current use of the double 'g' in Coggeshall.

An early version of 'The Visitors Guide to Coggeshall' written by Mr.E.Tyrell Green [2], records that the settlement

was named as being 'the nook or abode of Cogga in Saxon times'. Readers should note that the use of the phrase 'in Saxon times' could be taken as covering the period from around the 5th century up to and including the 11th century A.D. and that it was only from the 11th century that the Normans started to have an influence on English place names.
Morant notes in reference[3] that

> *"The name of this parifh is written in records thefe various ways. Cogfhal, Cogefhal, Cogefhale, Coggefhall, Coggafhael, Cokkifhall, Coxall, Coxhall, Goggefhale, Hoggefhall etc. The true and original feems to me to have been Cocks-hall"*

It is likely that such changes in the way of spelling the name of the town may have occurred due to an alteration in pronunciation and/or by the in-built propensity of some scribes to deal with spelling creatively. However it could also be noted that the coat of arms belonging to the now demolished Coggeshall Abbey featured three cocks, which some assume were intended to be a 'play' on the town's place-name. Unfortunately no early documents belonging to the Abbey of Coggeshall have been preserved,

Morant also records that the areas of both Great and Little Coggeshall were held 'in Saxon times' by a freeman called 'Colo' and at the time of the Domesday Survey by Eustace Earl of Bologne, when Great Coggeshall was then known as Cogheshala. The Manors were inherited by his only daughter Maud, who brought them by marriage to her husband Stephen the Earl of Blois, who subsequently became King of England. It was during his reign from 1135-1154, that the King and his Queen founded Coggeshall Abbey.

In common with many other towns Coggeshall was not immune to religious persecution. This was manifested in the reign of Queen Mary Ist (1553-1558), when it was deemed right that those of the Protestant faith should renounce their beliefs in favour of the newly resurrected Roman Catholic faith. Predictably this was merely a matter of expediency for some, but Thomas Haukes of Coggeshall was resolute in his continuing to be loyal to his Protestantism [4]. He was in the employ of the Earl of Oxford and as the son of a 'gentleman' he also attended the Royal Court. When his child was born he omitted to have it baptised immediately and this was seized upon by those who wished him ill, as a pressing reason to denounce him to his employer.

The Earl who himself had found it expedient to embrace the `new' faith, sent Thomas under guard to Bonner the Bishop of London, who specialised in taking extreme measures in order to eliminate religious dissenters. The result was that after several days of questioning Haukes was sent back to Coggeshall in the charge of Lord Rich and on June 10th 1555, in Vicarage Field which is north of West Street at grid reference TL 846 226, he was burnt at the stake. His house was in Market Hill opposite to the Chapel Inn. It is now known as Constantines and it currently houses a shop dealing in classical plaster mouldings. In the same year and in like manner Bishop Bonner also dispatched a 19 year old youth called William Hunter; this took place at Wilson's corner at Brentwood, where a memorial now stands to commemorate the infamous deed.

Coggeshall was at one time famous for producing jokes known as Coggeshall 'jobs', in which the recurring theme played on the supposed stupidity of the Coggeshall populace. The following three examples are typical of the genre.

Of two windmills sited in the same area at Tilkey, one was pulled down because there was clearly not enough wind to drive both of them.

The villagers were said to have hung a pair of wet blankets on a line across the road leading into the village, in order to keep out the latest infection.

The quality of Coggeshall recruits enlisted to fight in the

Napoleonic Wars was such that the only way to obtain the desired effect on the parade ground, was to fix a piece of hay to their left legs and a piece of straw to their right legs and then give the command 'hay, straw, hay, straw'....

More of the same standard with illustrative drawings can be found in 'Coggeshall Jobs' by Alison Barnes, Essex Libraries, Goldlay Gardens, Chelmsford. It would seem to be a fair comment that such material has over the years provided the feedstock for all those puerile 'Essex girl/boy' jokes, with which denizens of the County have traditionally been saddled and 'up with which we (seemingly) have to put'.

The following proverb relating to the area has been taken from John Ray's 1670 edition of his Collection of English Proverbs.

*"Braintree for the pure and Bocking for the poor,
Coggeshall for the jeering town and Kelvedon for the Whore".*

Why the citizens of Braintree should be classed as 'pure' does seem a little odd, perhaps it was based on their observance at that time of all things religious? Or could it reflect the fact that John Ray lived in Braintree. It is known that a contingent of Flemish immigrants settled initially in Bocking, so that Bocking probably could be said to have had accommodation which at that time may have been at the lower end of the market and could therefore be described as being 'poor'. To describe Coggeshall as a 'jeering town', was probably apposite in view of the plethora of Coggeshall 'jobs'; while for Kelvedon,- well, perhaps it had better be noted that the same proverb was quoted by E.Tyrell Green in 1931 in reference [2], in which the last line ran.....'Kelvedon for the boor'. Such a misquote was almost certainly deliberate and it is in the best tradition of Dr.Thomas Bowdler (1754-1825) who was instrumental in expurgating all words, expressions and plots, which could not with propriety be read aloud in a family. When so treated, such literature was said to have been 'bowdlerised' and of course the modern equivalent of this, pioneered by Mrs. Whitehouse is reflected in our concern that the subject matter of television programmes transmitted before the 9.00 pm 'watershed' should always be suitable for family viewing.

When the railway system was being built the inhabitants of Coggeshall did not want the town to be included in any such development; with the result that the nearest station is at Kelvedon and the resulting 'spin off' of economic development associated with the creation of the railway infrastructure did not occur in the area. The town was once famous for the intricate art of lace making and also for the manufacture of velvet. Gelatine and isinglass were once manufactured locally. Nowadays the town is known internationally for seed growing, for furniture and antiques and for clothing. It is also used as a dormitory town for commuters into London.

Coggeshall Abbey (ruins)

The Abbey was founded in 1140 by King Stephen and Queen Maud and it was sited on the South side of the river Blackwater. Because there is no stone suitable for building in the area the skills of brickmaking were brought from other monastic establishments on the continent. Initially the Abbey was occupied by men from the Order of Savigny, but in 1148 it was merged with Cistercian monks, who originally came from Citeaux in Burgundy. The Cistercian (white) monks were responsible for starting and nurturing the wool trade in the area. This flourished for about five centuries, with Coggeshall being one of the centres of excellence in Britain. Towards the end of this period during the reign of Queen Elizabeth 1st, the production of cloth in the region was given an added boost by an influx of Flemish workers, who were fleeing from religious persecution in the Netherlands. The Abbey flourished until the Dissolution of the Monasteries in 1538 when it was surrendered to the

Commissioners of King Henry VIII, after which most of it fell into decay.

Part of the Abbey complex was the Gatehouse Chapel of St. Nicholas which is sited on the north side of Abbey Lane. It was built circa 1142 partly from bricks manufactured locally in Tilkey, where in 1846 a kiln was discovered, which was constructed of the same type of bricks as those used in the Abbey buildings. According to E.Tyrell Green, the place name 'Tilkey' signified the 'Tile Kiln' and readers should note that the difference in meaning between 'tile' and 'brick' was not as marked then as it is today. Mr.J.S.Gardiner writing in reference[5] cites this chapel and the oldest of the remaining structures, as being representative of rare and fine examples of the early use of brickwork in the period after the Roman occupation, but before the 15th century, when the use of bricks became more common due to the influence of a trading group from Northern Germany referred to as the 'Hanseatic League'.

The Gatehouse Chapel is close enough to Coggeshall Hamlet to have served those residents until the time of the Dissolution, but reference [6] records that it was probably built as a rival church to that of Great Coggeshall. After the Dissolution it became neglected, being used as both a barn and a cowshed for approximately 300 years, until in the 1860's the Reverend W.J.Dampier bought the building. The restoration has since been completed and it is still used for services.

Some of the remains of the Abbey buildings can be seen to the east of the Chapel sited on the west bank of the mill stream. In 1581 a farmhouse was built on the site, which according to E.Tyrell Green incorporated an ambulatory with dormitory above it, together with another two storey building constructed at right angles to that, whose purpose he does not specify. East of this building and at right angles to it is a building referred to as the 'Monk House' which some consider to have served as an infirmary but which E.Tyrell Green suggests was the scriptorium. It should be noted that other authorities suggest different uses for the

Saint Nicholas Chapel - Coggeshall

same buildings. The foundations of the Abbey church are on the north side of the farmhouse and their outlines become visible only during a dry summer.

Predictably the Cistercian monks led a life which was strongly orientated to the observance of the scriptures. Over a 12 month period, each month was dedicated to studying a different part of the bible and to celebrating a different aspect of the life of Jesus Christ and, at the year's end, the programme was then repeated. The lifestyle of the order of Cistercian monks as described by Wilfred Turner in reference [8], tended to be agrarian and very practical rather than academic, with the result that their architectural and building skills were of a high order.

The monks retired to bed about 7.00 pm and rose at 2.00 am to recite Matins and Lauds and from then on until sunrise, the time was spent in singing the Offices and in meditation. At sunrise they proceeded to work in the fields, stopping only to sing one or other of the day Offices. No food was eaten until dinner at about 2.00 pm which was served in the monastery. This was followed by a rest period of 1 hour, after which they returned to the fields to work until sunset. After returning to the church one of their number would read aloud to the whole community and this would be followed by Compline and bed.

This prescribed existence was in later years relaxed somewhat, due to the monastery receiving gifts of land and becoming more prosperous. According to Turner, the white monks initially resisted the acquisition of land, in order to avoid receiving unearned income; but apparently it was considered difficult to refuse the largesse offered by Kings and nobles, who were attempting to 'buy' some religious respectability, as well as commanding that prayers be said on a regular basis on their behalf, probably for reasons best kept to themselves.

Life in the Abbey was regulated by the hourly tolling of a bell. The passage of time was measured according to the Roman system in 'temporal' hours. This system allowed for both daytime and night time periods to be divided into 12 hours. This meant that the period of time designated by one hour varied both by day and by night and also with the seasons. Hence during the day in the summer, one hour represented a longer period than it did at night, resulting in a longer time spent in the fields during the day and a shorter time spent in the Abbey at night; during the winter months the reverse was true.

It is interesting to consider the various ways in which the monks could have detected the passage of time. When the sun was visible a sundial could be used to determine the passage of equinoctial time, which with the use of tables could then be converted into temporal hours, so that when one temporal hour had passed the monk could then ring the Abbey bell. When the sun was not visible, It is probable that reliance was then placed on the rate at which a candle burnt down to a level as indicated on a set of suitably calibrated scales.

Dr. Whitrow [9], records that Vitruvius writing about 30 B.C. described a number of 'clepsydrae' or water clocks. Their principle of operation relied on water under a constant head flowing through an orifice, such that when a given volume (or mass), had passed, this indicated the passage of one hour of equinoctial time. Such hours were not of course temporal hours and this led to considerable complications in the mechanism of such clocks when temporal hours were required! Arno Borst writing in reference[10] reproduces a reconstruction of an elaborate water clock invented by Ctesibius of Alexandria in the third century A.D. which attempted to deal with this situation. In the late 12th century a guild of water clock makers existed in Cologne in a street called the Urlogengasse. The use of water clocks was mainly confined to the warmer parts of the globe, where no difficulties with the freezing of water were likely to be encountered.

In the 14th century the sand-clock or hour glass was invented, which overcame the drawback of freezing. These sand-clocks were mainly designed to measure the passage of relatively short intervals of time and it is possible that the monks found a series of uses for them in their daily lives. According to Dr. Whitrow sand-clocks were used principally on board ship to measure periods of half a minute, during which time a rope knotted at equal intervals and attached to a log was paid out. By counting the number of knots which had passed, the speed of the ship could then be calculated in knots/hour.

At the time of the Black Death in 1348, so many people died that those who were spared discovered that manpower was at a premium and that 'the labourer was indeed worthy of his hire'. In addition they probably found that it was more beneficial for them to be paid according to a fixed (equinoctial) hourly rate, than it was to be paid by the day, or by the job. This meant that at that time there was a pressing need for a device which would measure equal hourly intervals automatically and continuously and, it is around this time that the first mechanical clock was invented by a person (or persons) unknown. It is apposite to mention that the word 'clock' is derived from the French 'cloche' for bell, as initially the mechanism was attached to a bell, presumably with the object of saving the labours of those monks who were required to toll a bell on the hour. For those readers who wish to know more about the way our ancestors regarded and dealt with the passage and measurement of time and of the various ways in which calendars were contrived, references [9] and [10] can be recommended.

The Abbey Mill

The Abbey Mill House is a 15th century building which was extended in the 18th and 19th centuries. The original Abbey Mill built by the monks served as a flour mill. In the early part of the 17th century Flemish refugees rebuilt the mill changing its use to that of a 'fulling mill'. Later around 1820 it was changed again to operate as a 'silk throwing mill' by John Hall, who was an established manufacturer of silk ribbons from Coventry. In 1839 it was converted to corn grinding by Robert Bridge Appleford and subsequently bought by him in 1879. During this time Mr and Mrs Appleford took delivery of 10 sons and on the occasion of each birth a lime tree was planted in the grounds of the mill between the boathouse and the cottage. A recent storm has now reduced the number of trees to nine. In 1857 the machinery of the mill was adapted so that it could be operated using steam and according to reference [7] the mill ceased operations in 1960.

The conditions of employment offered by John Hall were such that the people of Coggeshall refused to allow their daughters to work for him and consequently he was obliged to 'import' his labour force which consisted of girls aged between 11 and 16. Mr.Hervey Benham quotes a newspaper report of 1825, when a group of 50 girls working in a mill in Hatfield Peverel walked out in protest at their conditions. One girl said she worked six days/week from 6 am to 7 pm with half-hour breaks for breakfast and dinner, for 3s 6d/week in the first year and 4s/week in the second. She then paid 1s/week for lodging and 2s 6d/week for food and had little to eat but bread. The report goes on to record that she was then sentenced to seven days hard labour! Clearly the 'dark satanic mills' referred to by William Blake (1757-1827) in his anthem 'Jerusalem' were certainly not a figment of his imagination.

Paycocke's House

The house was built early in the 16th century. John Paycocke died in 1533 and on the death of his wife Joan the house was then left to his son Thomas (the second) in 1555. The family income was derived from sheep farming and the manufacture of cloth and Thomas died in 1580. From 1584 to 1746 the house was owned by the Buxton family and in 1890 in the form of three cottages in a dilapidated state, it was sold for demolition. According to the Coggeshall Official

Guide, a local antiquary Mr G.F. Beaumont managed to get the sale cancelled and in 1904 the property was acquired by Lord Noel Buxton, a descendant of the previous owners. It was then restored to designs which were approved by Sir Edwin Lutyens and in 1924 the house was presented to the National Trust. Fittingly the carving of the oak front door panels takes the form of fluted folds of cloth.

Grange Farm and Barn

This was originally the Home Grange of the Abbey and the site contains the Grange Barn; which is assumed to have been built by the Abbey monks. Its timber frame and King Post roof are cited as one of the finest examples of early timber construction. Tree ring dating of the timbers sets the time of building as between 1143-1213. Other tests on the timber indicated a felling date some time after 1235, while yet another test dated a post as being from the time of 1130 ±90 years. The building was restored by the Coggeshall Grange Barn Trust in 1982 and it is now open to the public for viewing and for hire under the auspices of the National Trust.

Dick Nunn's Bridge

Dick Nunn's Bridge as well as having an interesting construction also has an interesting story attached to it. According to the Coggeshall Official Guide, Henry Nunn (who for reasons which no doubt were obvious at the time was always known as 'Dick'), was born in 1836 and while earning his living as a blacksmith in Swan Yard became a 'champion of people's rights'. In 1875 the existing footbridge across the Blackwater collapsed and the Lord of the Manor decided both to close the footpath and deny that a right of way ever existed across his land. This 'double whammy' was not appreciated by those who were accustomed to use the path

Dick Nunn's Bridge - Coggeshall

and 17 years after the event 'Dick' decided to do what he could to redress the situation, by constructing a new 30 foot span bridge in his own smithy. He made it in two halves and then on August 31st 1892 he had them transported separately to the site, where they were joined together to form the present bridge. As always such stories inevitably pose further questions such as why did he wait for 17 years before taking his action? Could it be that he had to wait for ownership of the Manor to be transferred to a new and perhaps more sympathetic owner? Interestingly on 31st August 1992 a group of walkers some of whom were dressed in the manner of those who were active 100 years ago 'walked' the footbridge, later taking refreshment in the adjacent football pavilion.

A pen and ink sketch of the bridge is included in this publication together with a coloured photograph featuring some of the Waltham Wanderers, who at the time were engaged in 'proving' both this particular walk and the bridge.

Stoneham Street

This street contains the Roman Catholic Church and the Christ Church, the latter being used by an amalgamation of the Baptist, Methodist and United Reformed Churches. There has been a Congregational community in Coggeshall since 1662 and the Society of Friends (Quakers), had a place of worship on the site of the present Library in 1692.

The Heritage Museum is housed in an annexe of St. Peter's Hall on the west side of Stoneham Street. It is staffed voluntarily and is open every Sunday during the summer months.

The Royal Oak Cottage (on the east side of the street opposite to the School Mews), was once the Royal Oak Inn. Further on down the road in the direction of the walk is the 'Olde House', which once saw service as the Black Horse Inn, from which in 1848, the 'Coggeshall Gang' used to terrorise travellers and the local inhabitants. It is said that to avoid

Some of the Waltham Wanderers 'Proving' Dick Nunn's Bridge - Coggeshall

capture the miscreants would move along the road from the Black Horse using the loft spaces of the adjacent houses as a 'rat run'. The Black Horse Inn was later known rather curiously as the 'Locomotive'. At this time locomotives and carriages were being developed and it was not unknown during the course of a journey for foolhardy passengers to move from one railway carriage to another. Is it possible that a knowing analogy was being drawn in calling the Inn the `Locomotive'?

The Clock Tower was reconstructed in 1887 and was made taller to commemorate Queen Victoria's Jubilee.

Market Hill

The Chapel Inn in Market Hill has taken its name from the Chapel which once formed part of the Market House sited at the junction of the roadways. On this same site lived a Sheriff of Essex and during the Peasant's Revolt in 1381 his house was attacked by the followers of Wat Tyler. Opposite to the Inn is 'Constantines' which was once the home of Thomas Haukes who was martyred at the stake for his religious beliefs. The property currently contains a shop specialising in classical plaster mouldings.

Market End

During the reign of Queen Elizabeth 1st the building in which the Post Office is now housed once saw service as a public house. The 'Old Wool Hall' has been incorporated into the White Hart Hotel and what some believe to be the oldest house in Coggeshall is on the corner of the block and it is currently in use as a Travel Agency.

Church Street

This Street contains many old buildings. Swan Yard is situated on the south side of the road and the house on the corner (adjacent to the butchers), is reputed to be one of the oldest houses in the town. In 1394 it was known as 'Herrings'. Swan yard once contained the smithy belonging to Dick Nunn and the shop currently operating as a butchers was once known as 'Plummers'; it operated as an ironmongers shop and its sign was that of a large sheet metal padlock which is one of the many exhibits in the Heritage Museum off Stoneham Street.

The Manse and the house next door with the carved frieze date from 1565 and opposite this is a 15th century house called 'Hutleys', which is next to 'Cockerills'. 'Cockerills' dates from the 16th century and was restored both in 1800 and in 1922. On the opposite (south) side of the street Coggeshall House has some impressive Tudor chimneys and was mentioned in the Manorial Court Rolls of 1492,

According to reference[11] the Woolpack Inn was built in the 15th century and at one time it was home to Thomas Lowery a dissenting Puritan vicar who was relieved of his Living in 1660. The building has operated as an Inn since 1708 and it is remarkable for the way in which its roof is constructed using an octagonal king-post. Some of the dates referring to the Inn differ from those given in reference [12].

St. Peter ad Vincula (St. Peter in chains)

The church is built on the site of what was once a brick built Roman building and construction is believed to have been carried out between 1080 and 1105. The wealth associated with the wool trade enabled the merchants of Coggeshall to build some grand houses and also to enlarge the church, making the size of the building similar to those at Thaxted, Saffron Walden and Chelmsford. Before the Diocese of Chelmsford was formed St. Peter's was one of the four churches being considered as being suitable for designation as a cathedral.

The early English font once did duty as a horse trough in Pattiswick before being retrieved from a nearby garden to be installed in the church in the 19th century! In 1940 during an air raid the church was bombed and the tower was demolished together with much of the nave. Rebuilding was carried out and the church was back in full use by 1956.

Details of Walk 10

Map required:
Ordnance Survey Pathfinder Map No. 1076 (TL 82)
Coggeshall and Earls Colne
1:25 000.
Starting and finishing point:
Paycocke's House West street,
grid reference TL 8474 2250. Free parking is available close by off Stoneham Street.

The prescribed walk following the red arrows.
Distance covered:
9.7 km (6 miles).
Duration of walk:
3 h 30 min. including a 30 minute break.
Condition of terrain:
Generally firm and relatively smooth but might be boggy at Horseshoe Hole between points A and B (see sketch map). Details of an alternative route are given in the subsequent text.

The shorter walk following the green arrows.
Distance covered:
3.2 km (2 miles).
Duration of walk:
1 h 30 min. including a 30 minute break.
Condition of terrain:
Generally firm and relatively smooth.

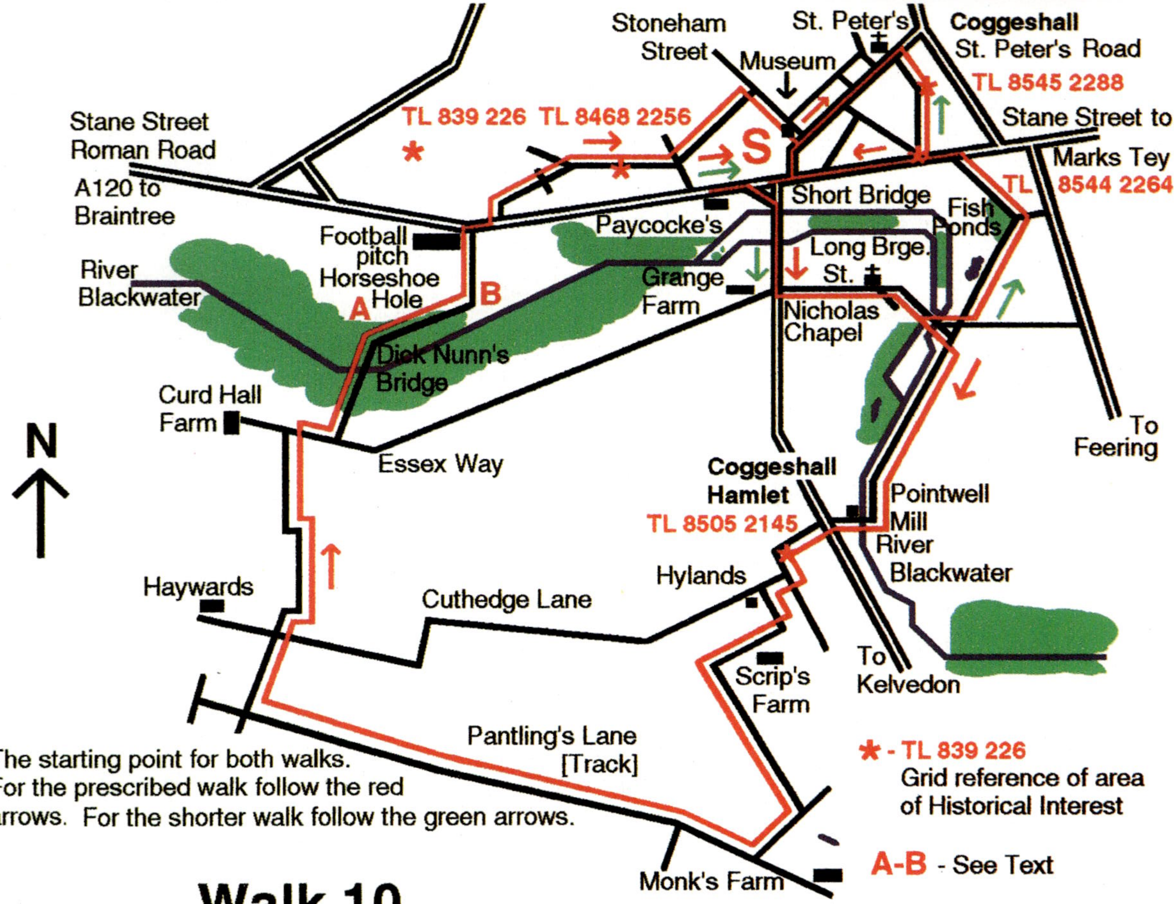

S -The starting point for both walks. For the prescribed walk follow the red arrows. For the shorter walk follow the green arrows.

* - TL 839 226 Grid reference of area of Historical Interest

A-B - See Text

Walk 10

Places of Refreshment:
In Coggeshall there is a wide choice of places of refreshment.

Both walks

Both walks start and finish at Paycocke's House. Walkers should move eastwards towards the road junction proceeding along the short section of street referred to as 'The Gravel', which leads into the aptly named Bridge Street. This passes over two bridges; the first one is called 'Short Bridge' and it crosses the original bed of the river Blackwater marking the boundary between Coggeshall and Coggeshall Hamlet where, according to Morant, a mill known as Tye-mill once stood in what was then called Tye meadow.

The second bridge is called 'Long Bridge' or 'Stephen's Bridge', (after King Stephen). It is carried on three 13th century red brick arches and it crosses a wider channel excavated by the Abbey monks in order to facilitate the operation of their mill sited further downstream. Like all mill pools its function was to make available a large volume of water stored at the maximum possible head, allowing the mill to operate for a reasonable length of time before the power available became too small for practical use.

On the approach to the second bridge on the east side of the road is Rood House, so called because in 1532 the Abbey granted Nicholas Crad Nicholas Crane a rood of land on which to build the house. Dr. John Gardner was born in the house in 1804 and he became the founder of the General Apothecaries' Company and the Royal College of Chemistry.

Also on the east side of the road is 'Monkwell', the lower central portion of which housed the Abbey Brewery. The brick lined well which supplied the water for this process is still in existence and it is located in what is now the garden of the house. According to the Coggeshall Official Guide, a man called Drago once lived there and he was responsible for introducing the art of making Tambour lace to the area.

The River Blackwater north of Pointwell Mill - Coggeshall

Grange Farm and Barn are situated at the top of the hill on the western side of the Kelvedon Road. The carved oak doorway belonging to the Grange is of Renaissance design.

Walkers should next turn eastwards, along Abbey Lane when on the North side, just before the lane forks, they will see St. Nicholas Chapel. Further on and down a slight slope is the farmhouse which was built in 1581 on the site of the Abbey buildings. Next the Abbey Mill House, Monk's House and Mill may be seen and it is at this point that the two sets of walkers divide. Those following the shorter route should turn left travelling in a north easterly direction, while those taking the prescribed route, should turn right moving in a south westerly direction. Separate directions for both walks now follow.

The prescribed walk

The footpath continues alongside the River Blackwater skirting wooded areas until Pointwell Mill is reached. This same mill was left to a John Doreward by his father in 1476 when according to Morant it was then called Pointell-mell. Later in 1776 on Chapman and Andre's map it is referred to as Pointer's mill. At grid reference TL 8505 2145 a Neolithic polished flint axe was found. This was on the south side of Scrip's Road at a point approximately 90 m from the junction of Kelvedon Road and Pointwell Lane.

The walk continues along Cuthedge Lane in the direction of Haywards. At Hylands House, (a point approximately 130 m along Cuthedge Lane), those walkers wishing to leave the Lane can take a slightly longer route towards Haywards (see sketch map), by taking the footpath leading in a south easterly direction to Scrip's Farm and Monk's Farm and joining with a track called Pantlings Lane.

Before reaching Haywards, both sets of walkers should then take the footpath leading in a northerly direction, subsequently crossing the Essex Way and traversing the woods before emerging into West Street (Stane Street) by the football pitch. The section of the walk between points A

Willow trees by the River Blackwater - near Pointwell Mill

and B on the sketch map is low lying and may at times be boggy. If this is found to be the case, after crossing Dick Nunn's bridge at point A, walkers should keep to the river bank until they reach point B. Alternatively they can return to Paycockes via the Essex Way and Grange Farm. A footpath leading northwards from Paycockes then leads into Vicarage Field and if required the designated walk may then be resumed.

During gravel digging Roman cremation urns were found in the area denoted by grid reference TL 839 226 (see sketch map), where it is thought probable a Roman cemetery once existed. Walkers should cross West Street and take the footpath leading in a north easterly direction, subsequently moving east across the Allotment Gardens (Vicarage Field). In this field Thomas Haukes was burnt at the stake and at grid reference TL 8468 2256 a prehistoric Neolithic unpolished flint axe and a bronze coin of the emperor Alectus were found. The footpath continues into Stoneham Street where walkers should turn right making their way into Market Hill, then turning left into Church Street leading into Church Green, where St. Peter ad Vincula is sited.

Next take the footpath on the opposite side of the road to the church, continuing in a southerly direction for approximately 130 m, where according to information obtained from the Town Planning Archaeology department [6], at grid reference TL 8545 2288, pottery dating from the late Bronze Age to the early Iron Age has been found; also tesserae, wall plaster and box flue tiles representing two phases of Roman occupation of a possible 'mansio type structure'. Phase one dates from the mid first century to the early second century and phase two dates from the second century to the early fourth century.

Continuing across the recreation ground to the junction of two footpaths and East Street at grid reference TL 8544 2264, pits and post holes have been found which indicate a supposed Roman site.

Walkers should then turn right proceeding along East Street in a westerly direction to return to the start of the walk at Paycockes.

The shorter walk

Walkers will have turned left just past Monk House and be travelling in a north easterly direction passing to the east of a reservoir. The path skirts a wood, on the western side of which the monks of Coggeshall once sited their fishponds. The position of these is marked on the sketch map and they are designated as being at grid reference TL 856 224. In the same area at grid reference TL 857 224 evidence of a brick/tile kiln, believed to have been associated with the Abbey have been found.

The path leads to East Street where walkers should turn west, subsequently taking the footpath leading northwards across the recreation ground towards the church of St. Peter ad Vincula. In addition to the church there are two points of interest on this section of the walk and they are described (in reverse order) in the last two paragraphs of the directions for the prescribed walk.

The last section of the walk is via Church Green into Church Street and the details of the various buildings passed en route have been given (again in reverse order to the direction of walking), in the sections dealing with Church Street and Market Hill.

References

1 Reaney P.H. Dr. The Place Names of Essex CUP 1969.

2 Green Tyrell E. The Visitor's Guide to Coggeshall (1931). Essex Record Office Box C8.

3 Philip Morant Reverend. History and Antiquities of the County of Essex 1768.

4 Jarvis Stan. Essex a County History 1993, ISBN 1 85306 245 6.

5 Gardner J.S. Coggeshall Abbey and its Early Brickwork. Journal of the British Archaeological Association Third Series Volume XVIII 1955.

6 The Archaeology Section, Essex County Council Planning Department, County Hall, Chelmsford.

7 Benham Hervey. Some Essex Watermills 1983 ISBN 09508919 08 Dewey 621.21.

8 Turner Wilfred. The Cistercian Tradition. Essex Record Office Box C5.

9 Whitrow G.J.Dr. What is Time?

10 Borst Arno. The Ordering of Time.

11 The Official Guide to Coggeshall. Essex Record Office Box C8.

12 The Coggeshall Branch of the W.E.A. 1974. A walk around Coggeshall. Essex Record Office Box C8.

Appendix A

Direction Finding

The problem

Sometimes a footpath branches into two or more other paths and the chances are that when this occurs, none of the routes are signposted. If also the terrain is such that it is not possible to see the next objective, due to adverse contouring, or because one is in the middle of a wood, or it has just become misty, then the walker is faced with the task of choosing which footpath to follow. Provided one can pinpoint one's position on a map, then with the use of the walker's compass it becomes possible to ascertain the direction in which to proceed.

The solution

Step 1 Pinpoint your present position on the map. Let this be point P. See Figure 1 (a) and note that it is not necessary to orientate the map.

Step 2 Pinpoint your proposed destination on the map and let this be point D.

Step 3 Place the straightedge of the compass along the line joining P to D.

Step 4 See figure 1 (b) and rotate the bezel of the compass until the north end of the parallel graticule lines (the red arrow), is pointing towards the top of the map and is parallel with the north/south grid lines on the map.

Step 5 See figure 1 (c). Lift the whole compass off the map and turn it either clockwise, or anti clockwise, until the north end of the compass needle is in line with the North on the bezel.

The direction of travel is then given by the direction of the arrow on the straightedge of the compass.

SUGGESTION

In order to become familiar with the method and to gain confidence in the results, the process could first be practised when the proposed destination D is visible and one's position on the map is known.

Note: If the direction given does not coincide with one or other of the branching footpaths it is just possible that the interpretation of your present position was not correct! In which case it might be considered prudent to consult your fellow walkers and to repeat steps 1 to 5, until a sensible answer is obtained.

As a last resort, if in spite of your best efforts, (and those of your enemies) all is still confusion, then modern technology can provide an elegant (though expensive), solution to the problem, in the form of a geo-stationary satellite linked to a hand held navigation device, which will pin point your position with an accuracy of ± a few metres.

A less expensive (though less accurate) electronic solution is now possible, using a mobile phone and suitable add-on hardware designed and tested by 'Cambridge Positioning Systems'. This system will produce grid reference figures on the display area of the phone, having the same degree of accuracy as the National Grid reference system, which is of course suitable for the needs of most walkers.

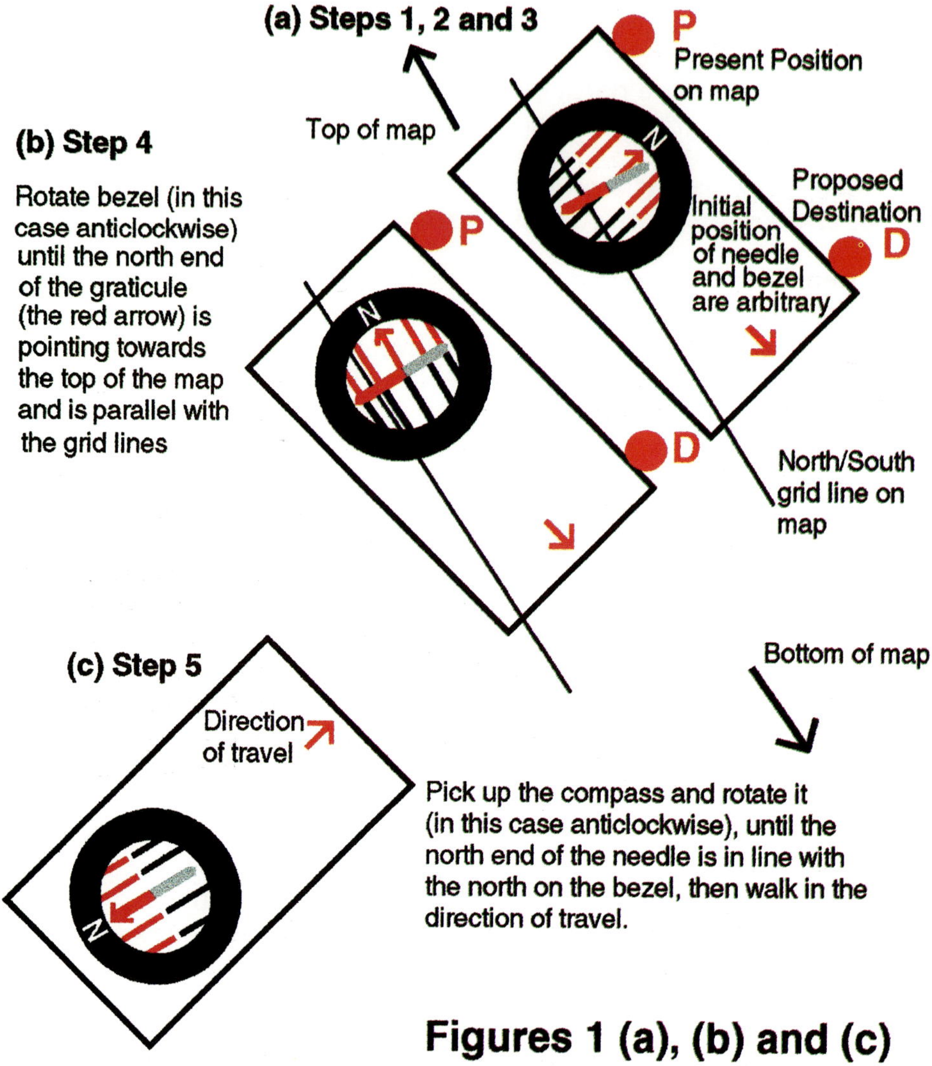

Figures 1 (a), (b) and (c) Direction finding

Appendix B

Use of the National Grid Reference System

Cartographers have divided mainland Britain into 100 km squares and each square is uniquely coded, using two capital letters. The code letters for the area dealt with in this book are TL and these letters will be found printed on each of the Pathfinder maps covering the area. Ordnance Survey of Southampton offer a free Index of their Pathfinder and Explorer maps, which also includes a chart showing the way in which the National Grid Reference System has been designated for use in mainland Britain.

Each Pathfinder map is itself divided into 1 km squares and these have numbers assigned to them, which for ease of reference, are displayed on all four sides of the map. Each 1 km square may itself be divided into 100 m squares using vertical and horizontal lines, but for reasons of clarity these lines are omitted; however an un-numbered scale dividing each 1 km square into 10 is printed along each of the four sides of the map.

EXAMPLE

To obtain the National Grid Reference for Great Waltham Church (see figure 2)

Step 1

In order to define the position of Great Waltham Church using the code, it is first necessary to determine the code letters designating the particular 100 km square in which the church is situated. Refer to the Ordnance Survey's free map index (which includes the National Grid Reference System), to discover that Pathfinder map No.1098 includes Great and

Little Waltham and that the area is designated as being in the 100 km square labelled as TL.

Step 2

The approximate position of the church on the horizontal (East-West) axis can be denoted by the numbers 695 which form the second part of the code.

Step 3

The approximate position of the church on the vertical (north-south) axis can be denoted by the numbers 134 which form the third and last part of the code. The position of the church may now be described as being approximately 100 m from the co-ordinate point denoted by TL 695 134.

Because the church at Great Waltham is a large and prominent building, it will obviously be recognised for what it is by those on site. However when attempting to describe the position of a smaller building, or perhaps the site of an archaeological dig, it is permissible to add a fourth number to the end of each of the second and third parts of the code.

For example the amended code for the centre of the symbol for the church may now be described as being approximately 10 m from the co-ordinate point denoted by TL 6954 1347.

PLEASE NOTE

ALWAYS quote the horizontal (eastings) numbers FIRST,

FOLLOWED BY the vertical (northings) numbers LAST.

A succint mnemonic makes use of the position of letters in the alphabet.

> ‘The letter E (for eastings), comes before
> the letter N (for northings)’.

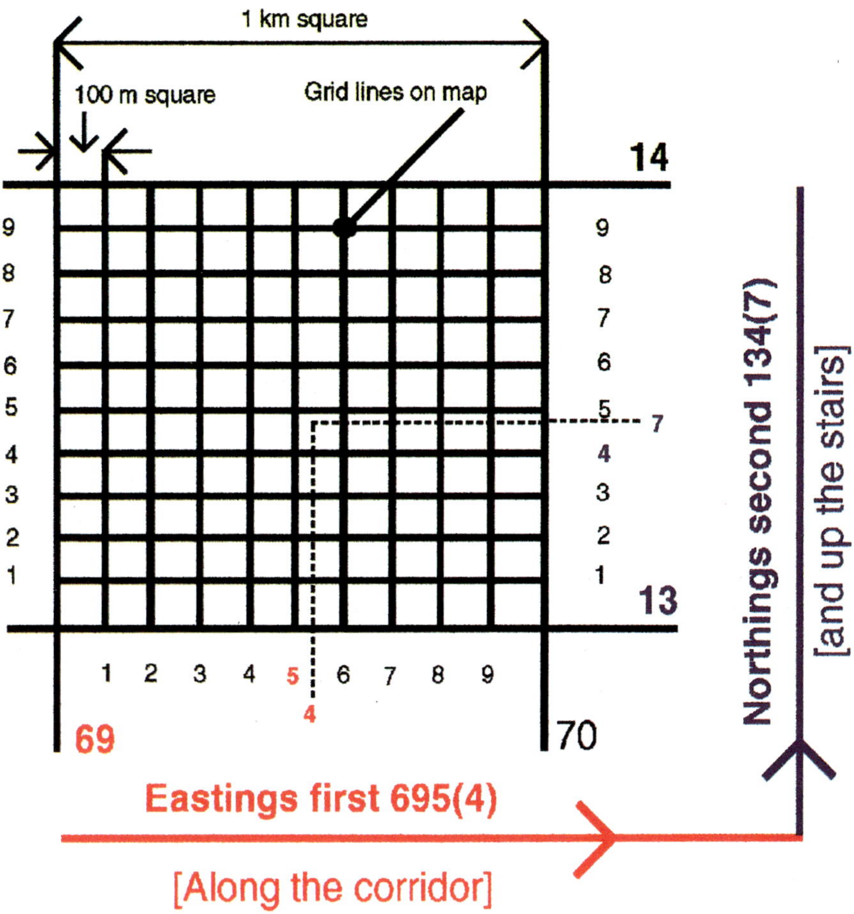

Great Waltham Church is approximately 100 m from the co-ordinate point denoted by grid reference TL 695 134

Figure 2 The National Grid Reference